127
Years of Design
1890-2017

The Michigan Daily

ALWAYS LEADING. FOREVER VALIANT.

Copyright © 2017 by Francesca Kielb
Some rights reserved

This work is licensed under the Creative Commons Attribution-NonCommercial-NoDerivatives 4.0 International License. To view a copy of this license, visit http://creativecommons.org/licenses/by-nc-nd/4.0/ or send a letter to Creative Commons, PO Box 1866, Mountain View, California, 94042, USA.

Published in the United States of America by
Michigan Publishing
Manufactured in the United States of America

ISBN 978-1-60785-430-2 (paper)

http://hdl.handle.net/2027/mdp.39015087418763

An imprint of Michigan Publishing, Maize Books serves the publishing needs of the University of Michigan community by making high-quality scholarship widely available in print and online. It represents a new model for authors seeking to share their work within and beyond the academy, offering streamlined selection, production, and distribution processes. Maize Books is intended as a complement to more formal modes of publication in a wide range of disciplinary areas.
http://www.maizebooks.org

The Michigan Daily

The Michigan Daily

U. of M. Daily

The U. of M. Daily.

The

U. of M. Daily

The U. of M. Daily

The Michigan Daily

The Michigan Daily

Michigan

The Michigan Daily

I would like to dedicate this book to the people who have made this project possible: Franc Nunoo-Quarcoo, Jason Colman, Gary Krenz, Anjali Alangaden, Shoham Geva, Emma Kinery, Shane Achenbach, Fritz Swanson, Carolyn Gearig, Michelle Phillips, Ava Weiner, and the many more staff members at *The Michigan Daily* who contribute to this publication's legacy.

CONTENTS

xi. Preface

1 The Masthead

13 The Front Page

43 The Redesign

PREFACE

Everyone says it: Print is dead. Newspapers across the country have been going through a process of intense change, as their primary method of distribution moves from print to digital. But my position as a managing design editor for The Michigan Daily means that I lay out the front page for the print version of a paper, design the layout of photos and the creation of graphics. I create the look of the paper, the feel of it. Looking at myself and my work for the Daily I wondered how many before me had toiled over that front page, and how few may follow. I was conflicted. I don't subscribe to the pure nostalgia some hold for the screenless days, when books were the primary source of information. While it's easy to dramatize the transition from print to digital using terms like death, I understood the very real benefits. What I didn't understand is how this transition would change my relationship with the design of the paper. Would seeing how many clicks I got on a page mean as much as seeing a stranger holding up the newspaper I had designed the night before? Is there a value shift when the paper ceases to be an object? Can I still say I made something? If I couldn't control what was happening, maybe I could at least understand it. Maybe if I could understand the ways that the paper has changed in the past with technological advance, then I could better understand my current predicament. I found some of those answers in a library basement with a bearded man named Fritz.

One of the Daily's copy editors had told me about the man who runs the printing press for the Wolverine Press, a letterpress shop operated by Fritz Swanson, a lecturer in the English Department. Apparently he had been there so long that when choosing his own uniqname and email he was able to pick whatever three letters he wanted. The editor told me he had showed her trays of old metal blocks of type, which they use to make books, and showed her how to use them. That's when I realized I had no idea how the newspaper was actually made. When I was finished designing at the end of each night I simply sent over the InDesign file to the printer, and when I woke up 10,000 copies just magically appeared on stands throughout the campus. I drafted an email to Fritz's three-letter address asking if he could take a few minutes of his time to explain printing presses and how they have changed since the Daily began printing in 1890.

At 10 a.m. on a Thursday, I wandered through the basement of the Duderstadt Library looking for Conference Room 100. The only people I know who go to a North Campus library are in the College of Engineering. Even though I am a senior, the space is dark and unfamiliar to me. The fluorescent lights flickered on the cement block walls. As I scanned the glass enclosed rooms lining the central space, I saw a black metal machine. It was an old letterpress. Smaller than I expected, maybe the size of a kitchen island, it was meant for personal, not industrial, use. I grabbed my pen and notebook and entered the room. Three people were engrossed in conversation, which I interrupted. They stared at me. There were two men and one woman. Each man had a beard — one, old and silver, the other, young and dark. Having heard the story about him being at the University for such a long time, I turned to the man with the silver beard and said, "I'm Francesca Kielb, from The Michigan Daily." He looked confused. The younger man stuck out his hand and introduced himself. "I'm Fritz."

The room was covered in shelves filled with tiny metal blocks. Each shelving unit was a different font, each drawer a different weight of a respective font (bold, bold italic, medium, medium italic, etc.) These were the types of building blocks used for all print materials created between 1450 and 1950. This small room in the basement library was transformed into a letterpress studio, which were once in common use, and the three people in the room facilitated this travel back in time.

When I mentioned that I was from The Michigan Daily, the woman, Rebecca Chung perked her head up. She said she was an editor at The Michigan Daily from 1985 to 1987. According to Rebecca, that period of time saw the greatest change in the way that the paper was made.

"One year we were using typewriters and the next we were using Macs," Rebecca explained to me. Her presence in this room suggested where her preference lay. I asked why, given the grueling process, she preferred the years she used a typewriter.

"Typewriter method allowed you and forced you to think concisely," she said. "Everything I learned about editing I learned from The Michigan Daily. We were brutal."

I thought back to the night before, which I had spent at my design desk, on one of the iMacs that populate the Daily's newsroom. Nights usually begin with a meeting of all the section editors. I find out from News which stories they want to put on the front page, and I talk with Photo about which images they want to highlight. I then confirm if we have any infographics or illustrations for the night, then oversee the design and layout of all special inserts. The night always ends with a call to the printers; after the articles have made their way through rounds of senior editors, managing editors and Copy; after I lay out the photos, place the articles on the front page and organize the spill; after the infographics and illustrations are exported as JPEGs so that they can be viewed online. After all of that, once the call happens, only four people remain in the room. I save the pages on one of the iMacs. The editor-in-chief dials the number. "Did you get everything?" she speaks into the phone. "The pages are all there? Great, have a great night!" She hangs up. Then she announces to the few of us left, "We made a paper!" Now, I imagined creating pages without our library of templates, without the ability to drag and drop, without auto-settings that ensure the text is always aligned and properly sized. What would my night have looked like?

Fritz pulled up a chair and began his story. It started with the letterpress. "You've worked in letterpress?" he asked. I gave a nervous laugh and said "a little bit." I have seen someone else print a poster once but never actually done anything myself. But in that moment it felt like a lie. Over email I made it clear I wanted to learn, but then, sitting in that basement in a wrinkled blouse, clutching my pen and notebook while holding up my recording app on my iPhone, I wanted to be taken seriously.

"It's a relief printing process. It's a recombinant process," he continued without skipping a beat, "What Gutenberg did that was special was he created a system for casting metal type and being able to rearrange it. You've seen metal type before? You've handled it?" "Yes," I replied, again stretching my single interaction with a press into some actual experience. I nodded a lot. He told me that while letterpresses had been used on smaller scales since the mid-1400s, newspapers were an 18th-century invention.

Imagine a room. You are a worker, surrounded by other workers and their trays. You place letter by letter by hand, forming words which eventually form paragraphs that eventually form columns that eventually form one page. You can smell the metal. And it gets worse. The whole page has to be laid out backwards in order for it to appear properly on the paper that gets pressed onto it — thus why it is called relief printing. So you are letter by letter forming an illegible inverse of the actual page, and if the tray is so much as slightly knocked during the chaos of the creation process, the tiny metal letters will fall and scatter onto the floor — and you will have to start from scratch. I'm struck by the physicality of it, people making something with their hands. To them, I imagine, what I do has nothing to do with the making of a paper. To them, I imagine, my work is so far removed that it might as well be displayed the way it was created — on a screen.

Fritz divides the newspaper's constraints at this time into three categories: labor, materials and time, or how many people can work in that space and for how long, how many sets of metal type can be bought and stored at one time and how quickly can the pages be assembled. The design of the front page is merely "a consequence of those pressures," he said. For example, the size of a newspaper today stems from the size that was convenient for one man to make in a mold in the 17th and 18th century. The sheet sizes were set by the manufacturer and were essentially determined by ergonomics — the largest size that was still manageable for a single worker to handle. Every change, every cut or adjustment to this set size was another added process, meaning added work and time. Making a paper that filled an entire sheet, then, was the most efficient and cost effective solution. As Fritz put it, it's "the reason why a newspaper is a newspaper, and not a news book. That is why magazines didn't come about until much later in the game. Thus 18th-century constraints have determined the sizing standards for an era with infinite possibilities." These conditions are why my InDesign file that I drag and click and arrange each night is the size and shape that it is. There is no other reason.

And it doesn't end with the paper size. Why is text arranged into narrow columns in newspapers rather than into a wider setting like books? There is a reason for The Michigan Daily's ultra-condensed, four-column design on its original front pages in 1890. On the tray where text was laid out there would be set galleys, or channels built up on the press to divide the words — metal lines of separation — making columns a norm in newspaper printing.

At this point Rebecca steps in. "When I was working at the Daily, I didn't realize it," she said. "But we had those cases, I had to send copy down by 6 o'clock at night, and then we had a typesetter named Lucius, Lucius Doyle, and he was grouchy and mean and tough and we loved him. Once he was done doing the hot metal setting, we would go look at it there and we would look at a print and we would make final decisions. The more metal involved, the fewer corrections he was willing to make."

She paused, recalling the year before they transitioned to the Mac.

"I had no idea that I cared about it so much while I was there," Rebecca said. "It was all just sinking in. But I'll let you two get back to talking."

She returned to her work setting up the new letterpress studio. Her self-realization prompted internal debate. Why do I care that the digital file I create gets duplicated 10,000 times on paper? Why does it matter that I can pick it up on my way to class and hold it in my hands? Why is that more meaningful to me than pulling it up on a screen? And lastly, will I care like she cares when it dies?

"I'm glad she brought that up," Fritz adds. "Because the Daily was still set — do you know about the linotype machine at all?"

I lie, laugh awkwardly and say, "A little."

I think he knows by now what my responses really mean, because he explains it anyway. He explains that columns such as ads would stay set up week to week to save labor. But in the meantime the rest still had to be constructed by hand — that is, until the linotype machine was made in the 1880s (though not broadly used until the early 20th century). Now, instead of hand placing each letter, you could use a typewriter. Each letter you pressed on the typewriter would prompt that same letter in real life, in metal block form, to slide down into a line on the newspaper tray. You could type a single line of text, then that text would be cast in metal together into what was called a slug. Now, say you trip and the tray spills on the floor. Instead of having tons of individual letters scattered everywhere, you had complete lines, formed together, which could be picked up and rearranged again back to the proper order. This one machine cut work time significantly.

This development explains why the column grid begins to loosen up in the early 20th century. The linotype was able to adjust the length of the lines (or slugs) that were cast, and therefore headlines begin to span multiple columns and graphics begin to enter into the designs because there was no longer hand-setting of pages. The efficiency allowed for flexibility. Yet it is important to note that, while minor changes have been made, papers continue to stick with essentially the same columns that were made 150 years prior.

Fritz paused. It had been more than 30 minutes and I apologized for keeping him from the letterpress. He told me he needed to get back to it soon, but wanted to finish the story. I looked up and saw the other two time travelers in the room, tinkering with the letterpress machine and organizing stacks of hand-printed papers on a table.

He finished the story.

"It was probably a roller manufacturer in the 1950s who

observed this effect first," Fritz said. "If you print onto a glossy surface — like plastic — then if you press that glossy surface back onto paper, it will deposit that ink."

The capability to print with ink on plastic meant that presses no longer had the restrictions of metal type, and paper could instead be rolled through cylinders and printed. This technique of drawing paper through cylinders meant that the paper could be fed much more quickly, further improving the efficiency of production.

Imagine you have been working a letterpress all of your life. You are accustomed to the metal blocks of type, the trays. You hold onto it for as long as you can, but eventually you just can't compete. Offset presses are taking over. They demand less labor, they require simpler tools and they take less time. It's a no-brainer. Fritz told me The New York Times, despite changing technology, printed on a letterpress until 1977. There was a video shot by one of the linotype operators about the last day of production on a letterpress. As I heard this, I sat there and wondered, is that heroic, to be the last to stick to a dying technology?

I was nervous to bring up the potential ecological benefit of print's death to a man setting up a letterpress, but I was curious to hear his perspective and surprised by his response.

"We are in a position now where you should only print things that you have to print — that must be in print … so how can we make this more utilitarian, more functional, more useful?" he said. "How can we leverage print so that we are not just echoing the past mindlessly?"

I didn't expect that from a man who has dedicated his life to print. Fritz knew that the cost of printing was high — not just financially. He was not of the mindset that business should just continue as usual, quite the contrary. His was a mandate: to understand the past and not press repeat, to ask questions and to print only that which must be in print.

But how do we determine what must be in print? Does our small, local, student run newspaper make that cut and — if so, why? Time passes, and the restrictions that originally demanded every design decision no longer exist, yet the conventions linger on, a remnant of technologies long buried. Print design may just be a remnant of history based on prior necessity, repeated blindly. Because, while I may have changed fonts, increased graphics and enlarged photos, there are still six, thin columns of text on our front page. Does that deserve to be repeated 10,000 times a day? When I got up to leave, Fritz went searching through the drawers and pulled out a small piece of cardstock. On it was every letter and number from his favorite font, Kennerley. He had set each letter of metal type, one by one, on the letterpress and printed it by hand. He reached out and gave it to me.

I held it in my hands. It was beautiful.

Article originally published by The Michigan Daily November 22, 2016.

• • •

THE MASTHEAD

1.
the highest part of a ship's mast or of the lower section of a mast.

2.
the title of a newspaper or magazine at the head of the front or editorial page.

1890

The University of Michigan's student newspaper, *The Michigan Daily*, was founded on September 29, 1890. As a student-run organization, the newspaper had to work within extreme fiscal limitations. It's first masthead displays the starting point for the evolution of the newspaper's brand. Unlike most professional newspapers at the time, which already used a standard gothic* font as a banner, the *Daily* used a hand-drawn illustration--perhaps to reiterate the from-the-ground-up nature of the project. The name '*U of M Daily*' was also subject to change. As a brand, this masthead sets a creative, while perhaps amatuer, independent tone.

* A heavy typeface (or a version thereof) in use from 15th to 18th centuries. Synonym: black letter.

1910

The Michigan Daily

The masthead in 1910 takes a wildly different direction. The structural serif* font gives the brand a more professional look than the illustration. However, it loses the essence of tree-spirit and creativity that was the driving feature of the masthead in 1890. *The Michigan Daily* has always stressed its editorial freedom, and prides itself on its ability to take stances that may question the authority of the University. The standard font and lackluster display evokes neither power nor freedom.

---

* A typeface with short lines stemming from the upper and lower ends of the strokes of a letter.

1920

The Michigan Daily

1920 marks a drastic change for the visual identity of *The Michigan Daily*. It abandons the basic serif font and adopts a more traditionally editorial gothic font for its masthead. While you will see alterations over time in size and spacing, the changes going forward are much more subtle.

1970

The Michigan Daily

Fifty years later and not much has changed. In 1920 print was booming and page sizes were getting larger and larger. By 1970 pages begin to grow gradually smaller and smaller and type becomes increasingly condensed. You will notice that the major difference between the two mastheads is the kerning* between letters, which is now significantly smaller.

* Adjusting the spacing between letters or characters in a piece of text to be printed.

2017

The Michigan Daily

While not much has technically changed with the masthead, the letters are crisper and more distinct. This can be attributed to the digitalization of all print media. The transition from printing press to printer, and from hand-laying of letters to the use of InDesign* for fonts and layout, means that the characters are both digitalized and exact.

* A desktop publishing software application produced by Adobe Systems.

THE FRONT PAGE

The front page of a newspaper displays the most relevant, noteworthy information each day. It sets the tone for the rest of the publication, and creates a brand for the paper as a whole. Since 1890, the size, use of photography, story placement, and general layout of *The Michigan Daily* has gone through waves of change. What is interesting to note is that this change has not always been linear. While some redesigns introduced entirely new ideas, incorporating methods of layout and design that were previously unseen, many other design changes were recursive, looking back to previous decades for inspiration for the future. That being said, while looking for inspiration for the most recent redesign of the newspaper, we believed that it was pivotal to look both forward and backward, to inform our future with our past.

U. of M. Daily

Volume I. MONDAY, SEPTEMBER 29, 1890. Number 1.

ROEHM
AND
--SON,--

MAKERS OF

FRATERNITY
PINS,

Woodward Avenue, Grand Circus Park,

DETROIT, - MICH.

FACULTY ANNOUNCEMENTS.

GENERAL BIOLOGY.—The undersigned will be in the Botanical Laboratory on Wednesday between 10:30 and 12:30 a. m., to consult with students about courses in Zoölogy, Botany and Morphology. Laboratory work in Biology begins Thursday at 9:30, in room 25.
V. M. SPAULDING.
J. E. REIGHARD.

LATIN.—Course 1. Section V. only, will report to Prof. Rolfe, will be limited to students who have shown exceptional proficiency. It is expected that this section will cover more ground than other sections.
Course 3. Section IV will be taken by Mr. Clement.

HYGIENE.—Students wishing to take the courses in Bacteriology will find Mr. Novy in Hygiene Laboratory every afternoon this week. An optional course in Water Analysis will be given this semester.
MR. NOVY.

ENGINEERING STUDENTS. — A course in Foundry Work will be given the first semester.

OUR RUGBY TEAM.

THE NEUCLEUS OF IT PRACTICING DAILY ON THE CAMPUS

The Campus has taken on a home like look this past week. Every afternoon has seen some of our canvas backed Rugby players tossing the ball back and forth, or trying to kick goals. It has been cold and raw, but the spectators have had many a laugh as the boys would form an invincible V and split the wind with it, but if they have had nothing but the wind to buck against, they have at least been learning to stand shoulder to shoulder. And they are doing good work, these few who are back getting in condition by tossing the ball, tackling, breaking the line, trying the V or the gridiron, and learning the twist that gave Ames of Princeton his celebrated nick-name of "Snake Ames."

The boys are working under Malley, who has brought back a trunk full of new tricks and has already began to teach his men a few of them. Abbott, Trainer, Hatch, DePont, Rathbone, Dygert, McAllaster, Stone, and Chadbourne take to them as naturally as any canvas-back does to water. Of course the boys are all "soft," and short winded as yet, but if they follow the liner laid down by Captain Malley it will be soiled meat and sand that Cornell runs up against this year.

It does one's heart good to hear before, and there will be a game at Buffalo this year that will be marked by sandy playing, and a much closer score than Cornell will look for. To begin with "Systematic Work" is to be the foundation of the Rugby eleven this year. At 4 P. M., every day, every man who wants to play on the *teams must* show up on the Campus. At 4:15 the players on the ground will be placed on the lines of the two teams—for it is Malley's intention to play two teams every day—and the players will play in these positions the remainder of the day, the late comers taking any positions that may be left (?) when they get there. At 5:15 the teams will go to a bath-room to be placed probably in the basement of the Medical building. Here a douse and a rub and then to Prettyman's, where they will rest and discuss the plays of the afternoon while a supper is being prepared for them at a training table that Prettyman is to run for them. This will be run in the same way that the Eastern training tables are.

"Those who work shall play." This comes pretty near being an Irish Bull, but Malley says that "It goes," and adds "I want at least fourteen new men this year, and I want the boys to come out and try for these positions. And when it comes to selecting the men who will go East this year, it is going to be a simple question of the twenty-two men who can and have been playing the best Rugby day by day. Twenty-two

---

Wright, Kay & Co

Foreign Buyers Importers of Gems and Art Goods, Jewelers and Opticians Manufacturers of the Finest Society Badges made in the country Samples sent upon proper references.

Detroit Opera House BP

140 WOODWARD AVE.,

Detroit, - - Michigan

---

they ever hope to down the Eastern team. And the fact is they got to work if they play this year."

Malley is very, very right, as every man who plays Rugby ought to come out, put his foot in the ball, and try for a position on the team. If you fail for the Varsity eleven there will still be the second eleven, all of whom will take the Eastern trip. Twenty-two men will go East.

In the way of material not already noticed Van Deventer, Shermans, Haynes, VanInwagen, Glidder, Sunderland, Duffy, and Prettyman are expected to be here this year. For new material Jewett, who played a rattling game as half-back for the High School eleven last year, enters lit. Ninety-four also gets Chadbourne, who played center on Phillip's Exeter Academy eleven last year, the eleven that made such a good showing against such college teams as Dartmouth, Amherst, and the Tech. Over in law school they have Stone, a graduate of Swarthmore, '89, who played full-back a portion of

1890

The Michigan Daily's first paper was printed on September 29, 1890. The page consisted of a four column grid* with small margins between the lines, with text pressed tightly up against each other. The masthead is hand-rendered and has a sketch-like quality. If you look to the ad boxes on the right and left corners, they combine hand lettering, serif, and sans serif* fonts. The layout is solely text based, with little to no visual diversity or differentiation.

✶ A structure made up of a series of intersecting straight (vertical, horizontal, or angular) guide lines used to structure content.

✶ A typeface without short lines stemming from the upper and lower ends of the strokes of a letter.

1900

By 1900, *The Michigan Daily* had adapted from hand-rendering to a traditional gothic font for their masthead, similar to those that were being used in larger newspapers. Their brand, however, was still in flux, titling themselves, '*The U of M Daily.*' Like 1890, the front page consists of four extremely dense, text-heavy columns. Subtle differences include the dedication of the entire far-left column to advertisements, showing an increase in popularity and profit gain. The advertisement column displays the greatest visual variance on the cover. Another difference is the inclusion of a large, bold serif font for the title at the top of each column, with a small, centered rule* dividing each headline from the decription and body text.

* A line indicating a division or beginning of content (like the line above).

The U. of M. Daily.

Vol. X. ANN ARBOR, MICH., FRIDAY, SEPTEMBER 29, 1899. No. 5.

WILD THE TAILOR

Fine Fall and Winter Suitings, Golf Suits, Fancy Vestings.

DRESS SUITS A SPECIALTY

We Carry the Largest Stock In the City.

108 EAST WASHINGTON ST.

WILD

BEFORE YOU BUY YOUR

DISSECTING CASES

Call and examine our 8 and 10 piece sets, in polished, hard wood boxes at $1.50 and $2.00, fully warranted.

WILDER'S
336 South State Street.

THE OLD RELIABLE For several weeks we have been laying in a stock for the boys, and now are ready with a full line of LUNCHES, CIGARS and TOBACCO.

PIPES A SPECIALTY.

R. E. JOLLY & CO.

DISSECTING SETS.

Complete sets, parts of sets or single instruments. We think we have exactly what you want and we know that the prices are right. Our cases for five instruments are very neat and convenient and were gotten up according to suggestions from Dr. Yutzy.

CALKINS, STATE STREET.

SECOND-HAND TEXT BOOKS

For all Departments, Law and Medical Books. Bring in your old books for exchange. College Stationery and Blank Books, all prices. Writing by the pound at 15, 20 and 25c. Make our stores your headquarters.

WAHR'S
Two Stores,
UNIV. BOOKSTORE,   DOWN TOWN,
S. State St.   Opp. Court House Main St.

HOW MUCH MONEY.

Should a College Student Have for the Best Success.

The Saturday Evening Post in an article headed "Earning an Education," has made a thorough examination of the cost of attending the leading universities and colleges of the country. The following questions were sent to the presidents of the various schools:

1.—In your opinion, taking all things into consideration, is the student paying his own way prevented thereby from accomplishing the best results?

2.—Is the unlimited supply of money likely to be a handicap to the average college student?

3.—Of two students having equal abilities, which has the better chance for college success, the one with much or the one with little money?

To the first question many replied emphatically in the negative, while others believed the student paying his own way is likely to be hindered from accomplishing the best results unless he be of unusual energy and mental and physical power.

There was practical unanimity on the second question, over ninety-eight per cent of those sending replies believing emphatically that an unlimited amount of money was a handicap to the average college student. Many believed it was worse than a handicap.

Along the same line as the opinion on the second question, the large majority believe that of two students of equal ability, the one having much money is likely to be less successful than the one having less.

The concensus of opinion is that the student depending entirely upon himself requires so much energy for outside work as not to be able to accomplish the best results. The one having just a comfortable allowance is the one who has chances most in his favor. The respondent from the University of Michigan is of the opinion that "above six hundred dollars a year is likely to be disadvantageous."

The following table gives the average and minimum expense and the attendance (last year's) of some of the leading universities:

INSTITUTION.	Average.	Minimum.	Attendance.
Williams College	$700	$250	385
Bowdoin College	340	250	284
University of Kansas	200	75	1100
Northw'n University	319	219	2942
Univer'ty of Michigan	300-400	250	3100
Beloit College	300	200	417
University of Vermont	300	200	554
Oberlin College	195-309		1084
Indiana University	150-300		1049
Univ. of Pennsylvania	400	335	2834
Boston University		300	1500
Harvard University		300	3901
Univ. of California	200	160	2300
Princeton University	250-1000		1100
Georgetown Univ.	500	400	700
Washington and Lee University	225-250		100
University of Nebraska	225	100	1915
Univ. of Tennessee	260	140	595
Purdue University	150-200		1750
Syracuse University	250-350		1200
University of Illinois		200	1750
Cornell Univ. (N. Y.)	400-500	160	2324
Univ. of Wisconsin	320	125	1920
Brown University	265-890		925
University of Iowa	224		1200
Minnesota State Univ.	300	200	2900
Ohio State University		200	1100
Leland Stanford, Jr., University	300	150	1200
Univ. of N'th Carolina	203	160	487
Dartmouth College	350	250	694
Yale University	545	350	2500

Changes in Football Rules.

The Intercollegiate Football Rules Committee held a meeting recently with the idea of making clear several points in the new code of rules drawn up last year. No radical changes have been made in the methods, but the rules as they now read cannot be misunderstood. Rule 7, that relating to the heeling down of a "fair catch," has been changed to read as follows:

"A fair catch consists in catching the ball after it has been kicked by one of the opponents and before it touches the ground, or in similarly catching a punt out by another of the catcher's own side. Provided the player while making the catch makes a mark with his heel and takes not more than one step thereafter. It is not a fair catch if the ball, after the kick, was touched by another of his side before the catch. Opponents who are off-side shall not interfere in any way with a player attempting to make a fair catch, nor should he be thrown to the ground after such catch has been made unless he advance beyond his mark as explained."

In rule 11, referring to the ball when "dead," it reads as changed.

"Should the ball strike an official, it is not regarded as dead, but play continues exactly as if the ball had not touched him."

Rule 28, dealing with penalties for fouls and off-side plays, has been changed. Section E has been made to read as follows:

"In case of a free kick (Rule 2f), if the kicker advances beyond his mark before his chasing the ball (Rules 7 and 15 b), whether he then kicks or not, the opponents shall be allowed to line up five yards nearer the kicker's mark, and the kick shall then be made from the same point back of the first mark, and at the same distance from the side lines. This shall also apply when the side having a free kick allows the ball to touch the ground and then fails to kick it, kick off and try at goal after touch-down excepted. The same ruling shall be given in case any player of the side making a free kick is ahead of the ball when it is kicked."

Section F of the same rule, which restricts starting before the ball is put in play for a scrimmage, provided there is no infraction of Rule 10, the ball shall be brought back and put in play again. If this occurs again in the same down, the ball shall be given to the opponents. If again during the game that side again infringes the rule bearing on this act, the ball shall be immediately given to the opponents. The same ruling shall be made in case of infraction of Rule 18, b and c.

Yale's New System.

Yale is trying a new system of football practice this fall. As in former years the Varsity and college elevens are retained, but in addition there are two other elevens which will play against each other and on these the new men will be tried, being promoted later, if their work is good, to the college eleven and thence to the Varsity.

Varsity vs. Hillsdale—College vs. Ann Arbor High—Saturday, Sept. 30, at Regents Field. Admission, 50 cents.

SCRUB TEARS UP VARSITY

Yesterday's Practice Will Cause a Shifting Around.

The second team heretofore known as "Scrubs" earned for themselves yesterday the more dignified eastern title of "College team," and as such, says Coach Fitzpatrick, they shall be known. The way in which the proteges of "Long" Allen made holes in the Varsity line and pushed through them until the goal line was reached twice has set the coaches on edge and there will quite likely be considerable shifting about in the Varsity line before they regain their natural equilibrium.

The practice was quite prolonged and several men were tired out, but the personnel of the two teams remained for the greater part of the play as follows:

Varsity.		College.
White	l. e.	Johnson
Wilson	l. t.	Juttner
Welz	l. g.	Howell
Dickey	c.	Kramer
Siegmond	r. g.	Kelley
Steckle	r. t.	Larsen
McDonough	r. e.	Martin
Gardner	q.	Herz
McDonald	l. h.	McAffee
Sweeley	f.	Keena
Durant	r. h.	Weeks

The Varsity scored first on a fifteen yard run by Sweeley through the line. But after this the College team kept the ball in the Varsity's territory nearly all the time. Once they lost for downs within a yard of the goal line, and twice they scored by hard plugging through the line. McAffee won much applause from the spectators by the way in which he tore things up in bucking through guard and tackle and in circling the ends. Herr at quarter-back did good work also. He is a new man whose experience has been gained at Villa Nova college. After being scored on, the second time the Varsity, by the aid of the kick-off and a blocked kick, immediately following, succeeded in tieing the score.

Coach Henninger declares that it is still too early to get much of a line on the men, and Coach Ferbert thinks that there will be considerable shifting around before anything that will resemble the final line-up of the season is reached. In fact he was not well pleased with the Varsity's showing yesterday.

An Old Alumnus Visits Law Department.

Judge Smith, 68L, of Lansing, visited the law department today. When he visited the law department yesterday. When he visited the second year class in equity jurisprudence, Dean Hutchins asked him to speak to the class. He spoke entertainingly of the work in the law department thirty years ago. At that time the course consisted of but two years of six months each, and was and counted one of America's best. By able jurists conducted the work, Judges Cooley and Campbell being then on the faculty. He closed by paying a tribute to the law school for its substantial progress and advancement, and for being now as then within the reach of all.

The DAILY will be free this week.

The Michigan Daily

Vol. XXI.   ANN ARBOR, MICHIGAN, SATURDAY, OCTOBER 8, 1910.   No. 5

FOGG'S MEN HERE READY FOR BATTLE

Hard Game Expected in Spite of Bear Stories from Case Headquarters

VARSITY IN GREAT CONDITION

	Michigan.	Case.
1894	18	8
1898	23	5
1899	28	6
1900	24	0
1901	57	0
1902	48	6
1903	31	0
1904	33	0
1905	36	0
1906	28	0
1907	9	6
1908	16	0
1909	3	6

Chapter fourteen of the above history will be recorded on Ferry field this afternoon when the curtain will be rung up on the 1910 football season, with Case as the varsity's opponent. At half past two o'clock, Michigan's supporters will have for the first time an opportunity to see in serious action the eleven which gives promise of being one of greatest that ever supported the maize and blue. They will also see for the first time the latest edition of "new football."

The varsity eleven is in excellent shape for the struggle with the Buckeyes and despite the absence of two of the strongest players is confident of making a splendid showing. The coaches drilled the squad hard behind closed gates yesterday afternoon, smoothing out the rough places and getting the offensive machine in the best working order.

CASE CLAIMS WEAKNESS.

Case's hopes and expectations may be gathered from the following special to THE MICHIGAN DAILY:

By Russel B. James, 10 L.

Cleveland, October 6.—The Case football squad, eighteen strong, together with Coach Joe Fogg, leaves Cleveland tonight at ten-forty-five for Ann Arbor for the annual opener with Michigan. While this yearly battle with the maize and blue is not looked upon as a game of local importance, much interest is aroused by it among students at Case, and, in fact, at all of the Ohio schools of equal calibre, as it is pretty apt to show what Case is to do later in the season when the Ohio "Big Six" championship is at stake.

The usual "bear stories" are afloat, some of which seem to have foundation. Tuesday it became known that Captain "Larry" Twitchell, who has been playing half, is "in bad" with the faculty and may not get in against Yost's gridders. Unless the faculty ban is removed Joe Slater will start at right half Saturday. Both of the ends are laid up with injuries. McComber has a badly wrenched ankle and Hird is out of the game with a fractured jaw. To add to this, tackle Glazer, who sustained a week ago in practice, has been forbidden by his physician to play again.

The quarterback job has given Fogg much trouble, no man having yet appeared who could combine speed with enough headwork to keep the team going. It looks like Goss or Gardner, who played on the Freshman team at Dartmouth two years ago.

LINESMEN LACK EXPERIENCE.

Heller, who has been seen on Ferry field before, will play fullback, while Roby will probably play opposite Twitchell or Slater at half. "Tiny" Abbott, another veteran, will be seen at center. Prochaska, Rosendale, Weller and Wilson complete the line, which for the most part, is composed of green men, whose worth is yet to be proved.

Case students do not anticipate a victory or even a scoreless game. Captain Twitchell said Wednesday that a thirty-six to nothing score would not surprise him, if the reports of Michigan's strength were true. At the same time, the Scientists have, and always have had, a fairly earned reputation for aggressiveness and grit, and it is likely that to roll up such a score as that suggested by Twitchell, Michigan will have to exert herself to the utmost.

CLEVELANDERS BOAST A GIANT.

Case has one man out every night beside of whom even Benbrook would look small. He is Elmer Fix, a sophomore, and he tips, or rather strains, the scales to the extent of 315 or 330
(Continued on Page 2.)

"PAY FEES PROMPTLY"

The above is a view of students waiting in line, endeavoring to obey orders and "pay entrance fees promptly." In some cases students stood in line for hours, reaching the door at noon, just too late to get in. They were compelled to return after lunch and take their chances with the new line.

On two of the days when such lines were formed, struggling for entrance, it rained. Some were forced to flee for shelter. Others, women as well as men, took their drenching as pleasantly as they could.

Thousands of dollars were spent by the university this summer in giving better facilities to instructors, creating offices, remodeling lecture rooms, etc. Nothing was done at the treasurer's office to improve this fee paying plan, though it fell under criticism last year. Not even were benches offered in sufficient numbers to the women.

MICHIGAN UNION PACKED TO DOORS

President Hutchins Emphasizes the Necessity of a Much Larger Clubhouse

BIG CAMPAIGN ENDS TONIGHT

Packed to the doors, the Michigan Union clubhouse saw the biggest night of its history yesterday. Dozens of men were turned away for lack of room President Hutchins, Dean Reed, and many other members of the faculty were present to shake hands with the undergraduates.

Working his way out of the crush, Prof. H. C. Adams remarked to Reception Committee Chairman Riordan, who was extending the "glad hand" at the door: "This is the best argument you could have for a new clubhouse."

While "Ike" Fischer's eight-piece orchestra served up catchy music in the dining room, one hundred gallons of cider were being consumed about the famous round table. Thirty men signed as members during the evening. Though the membership campaign will not be concluded until midnight tonight, the number of members is larger at present than at any time last year.

Speaking of the affair President Hutchins said, "What I have seen tonight shows that the Michigan Union is a necessity, and that you must have a very much larger clubhouse."

PROF. J. B. DAVIS.

Prof. J. B. Davis, for years a teacher of civil engineering in the university, has resigned. His resignation was accepted by the Board of Regents yesterday.

This faculty man graduated from the engineering department in 1868. For some years he followed his profession, and then returned to Michigan as an instructor. He was later made a professor.

STUDENTS CHEER OSBORN

Regent Gets Most Enthusiastic Welcome of Career

Yells and whistles, speeches and songs, roaring, ear-splitting enthusiasm, stereopticon pictures, men in the public eye, a willing hand, and almost 3,000 Michigan undergraduates—all these went to make the first mass meeting of the year, held in University hall last night, a tremendous success.

After Lyndon's stereopticon pictures of the team had brought enthusiastic bursts from the crowd, Wm. B. Hurvey, presiding officer, made a few remarks and turned the cheering over to "Cap" Haskins. The new field song, under the direction of Bob Bazley, was sung for the first time.

Judge H. Wirt Newkirk spoke interestingly of Michigan's past gridiron ethics. He was followed by Dean Jean M. Bates of the Law Department who emphasized the value of clean athletics. Hon. W. W. Wedemeyer made a few short remarks and gave way to Hon. Chase S. Osborn.

Almost unprecedented enthusiasm greeted Regent Osborn. Though being murred by just having passed through an 800-speech campaign, Mr. Osborn was momentarily unnerved by his reception. Recovering himself, he proceeded to set the crowd wild with one of his short characteristic speeches.

The singing of "The Yellow and Blue" closed the program.

WET COURTS KEEP TENNIS MEN IN.

The continued rains left the Ferry field tennis courts in such shape that it was found impossible to start play in the fall tournament on Friday afternoon. The tourney has been indefinitely postponed.

MONEY ON HAND FOR AUDITORIUM

Executor of Arthur Hill Estate Prepared to Pay Money Left to University

REGENTS MEET CHINESE BOYS

The Board of Regents and twenty-two Chinese students of the university sat down together at lunch yesterday in McMillan hall. Jack Wong, a senior engineer, made a speech for the students of the Orient, and a number of regents gave short talks.

Immediately after lunch, the Regents adjourned to their room for their monthly meeting. A most interesting letter to President Hutchins from the United Steam Engineers of Detroit, was read to the Regents. They asked for the supervisory direction of the engineering department of the university on their efforts along educational lines, and asked that a course of lectures in practical steam engineering be given before their meetings during the coming winter. The Board referred the letter to Dean Cooley, who favored the idea and said that men would probably be detailed from the faculty to deliver the lectures.

The executor of the Arthur Hill estate sent a notice that the estate was prepared to pay over the $200,000 left to the university for an auditorium. Regent Clements has been instructed to look up plans for an auditorium.

The matter of a new sanitary cement floor for the basement of the gymnasium was laid on the table.

It was decided that the News Letter should be reorganized, making it more truly representative of the university. It will probably be published in connection with the course in journalism.

A scholarship of $55 offered for the architectural course by the Michigan Chapter of the American Institute of Architects was accepted with thanks.

The more important of the appointments made were as follows:

Victor R. MacLucas was made assistant professor of law, to carry on the work of Professor Brewster while he is absent.

Clayton W. Bedford, B. S., was appointed assistant in chemical engineering; Arthur J. Decker instructor in civil engineering; George E. Wallace instructor in mechanical engineering; T. Cope, a graduate of Pennsylvania, instructor of mechanical engineering; Alfred H. Lovell, a Michigan graduate who has had considerable practical experience, in electrical engineering; M. N. Menefee, in descriptive geometry, and drawing; Franklin Thomas and Harry A. Angenblick, a graduate of Cornell, in descriptive geometry. A number of degrees were granted.

The next meeting of the Board of Regents will be held on November 18.

QUARANTINED PROFESSORS BACK.

Professors J. C. Knowlton and J. A. Craig, who had been quarantined in New York harbor because a few steerage passengers on their ships were suspected of having cholera, have returned to Ann Arbor.

More Ticket Sellers Wanted for Students' Lecture Association!

1910

1910 marked several major stylistic and layout changes for *The Michigan Daily*. First, they changed the masthead title to '*The Michigan Daily*,' and switched from a gothic font to a simpler serif font. Next, they expanded from four columns to five, beginning each column with a headline, rule, description, and body text. They then pushed the advertisements down to horizontal boxes at the bottom of the page. Furthermore, this is also the first implementation of photography in the cover's design, placing a vertical photograph in the second column, then a round photograph in a square box that consumes the lower portion of the third and fourth columns. Finally, this is the first example of columns being divided by a horizontal, not just a vertical, rule.

1920

In 1920, *The Michigan Daily* looked both forward and backward for inspiration. The masthead kept the title from 1910, but went back to the gothic style of 1900. *The Michigan Daily* continued to expand, adding a sixth column to the front page. They completely did away with advertisements on the front page, and packed all six columns full of content. They removed photography from the design layout to allow for a greater number of stories to fit, and included multiple stories in a single column with the use of a horizontal rule serving as a divider. In a space-saving attempt, they introduce a tall, condensed sans serif for headlines. Yet the visual identity is still a bit disorganized, using several variations of serifs and sans serifs, alternating size and italicization.

THE WEATHER
PROBABLY UNSETTLED WEATHER TODAY

The Michigan Daily

ASSOCIATED PRESS
DAY AND NIGHT WIRE SERVICE

VOL. XXXI. No. 8. ANN ARBOR, MICHIGAN, WEDNESDAY, OCTOBER 13, 1920 PRICE THREE CENTS

CLEVELAND TAKES SERIES, WINNING FOURTH STRAIGHT

ONLY TWO BROOKLYN PLAYERS REACH SECOND BASE

STANLEY COVELESKIE BRINGS TEAM SUCCESS

Robinson Praises Wonderful Team Work of Cleveland Organization Throughout Series

(By Associated Press)

Cleveland, Oct. 12.—The Cleveland merican League club won the supreme title in baseball here this afternoon, when the Indians defeated the rooklyn Nationals in the seventh and eciding game of the 1920 series, by score of 3 to 0.

Tonight Cleveland is celebrating in manner adequately in keeping with e honor, and it is doubtful if a overnment proclamation announcing e selection of this city as the future apital of the United States would eate a ripple of interest among the enzied fans.

Coveleskie Star Pitcher

The shutout victory was chiefly engineered by Stanley Coveleskie, the otball ace of the local team, who s proved to be a pitcher of remarkle skill and endurance during the ries. Backed by air tight defense on e part of his team mates at critical oments of the game, Coveleskie let e Robins down with five hits. Only o Brooklyn players reached second se and only five of the invaders were ft on bases.

Coveleskie's feat, in winning three the five games necessary to clinch e championship, will go down as one the outstanding features of world ries victories.

Indians Deserve Championship

In the shutting out of the Nationals in the final game this afternoon e Indians, led by Manager Speaker, se to playing heights which bore out e complete confidence of the club ckers and fans in their ability to ove their right to wear the basell palm of the universe. They ached the spitters of Burleigh imes, the National league hurlers, r seven hits; clinched their game fore the half way mark, and topd the play with several pieces of seball strategy that has marked the am as a championship organization.

"Cleveland has a wonderful ball club d Tris Speaker and his men cernly deserve the splendid support ey have received from the city," ilbert Robinson, manager of the ooklyn Dodgers, manager of the s a well fought and earnestly play- series. We did our best but we uld not hit the Cleveland pitchers."

ter the game it was announced by e national commission that the paid endance was 27,525, the largest of y of the seven games. Receipts re $82,906.

Library Showing Specimens of 18th Century Writings

Books from the Library's collecns of English dramatic literature ve been placed on exhibit for seval weeks in the main corridor of the neral library. The exhibit is pland primarily for the educators who ll be in Ann Arbor for President rion L. Burton's inauguration and o for showing the scope of the amatic collection of the 18th cenry in the Library.

Facsimilies of early plays by akespeare's predecessors and by akespeare are being shown. Severcases are devoted to Shakespeare, hibiting editions of his works, ncordances, and adaptations.

Another case is devoted to books th the lives of famous actors of the h century. One book written in 1 is for the instruction of young

Former Professor Dies In Colorado

James H. Brewster, Ph.D., LL.B., former professor in the Michigan Law school, died in Denver, Colo., Oct. 7, according to information received by Dean Henry M. Bates of the Law school. A general breakdown was given as the cause of death.

Professor Brewster, a graduate of Yale university in 1877, took his LL.B. in 1879, and went to Detroit to practice law. In 1897 he was made a professor of the law of conveyancing in the Michigan Law school. During his time at Michigan Professor Brewster wrote a book, several magazine articles, and did considerable other investigation work.

Developing tuberculosis in 1910 Professor Brewster left for the West, where he practiced law in Colorado for four years until he felt strong enough to assume a proffered position as professor in the University of Colorado law school. After a year there, he engaged in private practice in Denver until the time of his death.

Dean Bates, speaking of Professor Brewster while in the University said "Professor Brewster was a sound, scholarly man with a keen analytic mind that made him an expert in his field. His inspiring personality was a factor recognized by all who came in contact with him and made him a man both popular and respected in the Law school."

At the time of his death, Professor Brewster was making an indexed digest of the first 19 volumes of the Michigan Law Review.

INITIAL MEETING OF COUNCIL TO BE TONIGHT

MANY IMPORTANT MATTERS TO BE TAKEN CARE OF BY BODY

The Student council will hold its first meeting of the year at 7:15 o'clock tonight in room 306 of the Union.

The president hopes to get a line on the work of each of the members for the coming year at this time so that the various committees may be appointed as soon as possible. All members are requested to be present.

There are several important matters that must be taken care of at once by the council, among which are Traditions day, the pep meetings for the Illinois and Chicago games, fall games between the two underclasses, freshman conduct, and campus activities in general.

The president wishes it understood that the council desires at all times to serve the best interests of the campus, and he wants all students to feel free to offer suggestions.

MANY TO VOTE BY ABSENT BALLOTS

More than 250 students including 25 girls have sent home their applications for ballots and many of this number have also registered by mail, a representative of the Republican club stated yesterday afternoon. This club furnishes free the necessary blanks for all students who wish to vote by mail.

It has been estimated by the club that there are 2,000 student voters here from the states of Ohio, Indiana, Illinois and New York. Since these states are the crucial ones in the presidential campaign this year, the club feels more than justified in making the effort to poll these votes.

Many able speakers are being selected at the present time to come here to address the students in the near future, said a representative of the club. He stated that meetings would be held soon, the first probably next week.

ASTRONOMY STORY HAS NO BASIS PROF. HUSSEY STATES

Prof. W. J. Hussey, of the astronomical department, states, in an announcement in today's Official Bulletin that the practical demonstrations and engagement of instructors to take care of this work as appeared in a story in The Daily of Saturday is con-

GREEK, 15 YEARS OLD, YOUNGEST FRESHMAN

Spiros Vinieratos, '24E, only 15 years old, is the youngest freshman on the campus. He completed the work in the gymnasium in his home town of Argostoli, on the island of Cephallenia, Greece, and came here to study marine architecture.

His father, mayor of Argostoli, came with him as far as New York, but from there he came alone. Vinieratos has had only two years of English at his home, and although he can read quite fluently, he has difficulty in understanding the lectures. He has no friends or relatives in America, but he expects to remain here during the four years of his course, before he returns home.

LAW SCHOOL GRADS PASS BAR EXAMS

Every Michigan Man Passes Rigid Tests Given Recently by State of Illinois

LOCAL DEPARTMENT RATED HIGH AS RESULT OF SHOWING

Figures showing the efficiency of the Michigan Law school have recently been received that place the work done here far above that of the majority of law schools.

Illinois Record Good

In the recent Illinois state bar examinations, in which men from law schools all over the country took part, there were 400 men who took the tests. Of this 400, only 37 per cent passed, this percentage being a fair average according to officials, and it is not exceptionally low. The striking fact about the examination was that every Michigan man who took the examination passed. Advices report that several of the Mid-West law schools were hard hit by the showing of their men.

In the Ohio state bar examinations this fall the percentage of those passed is not available, but the reports show that all Michigan men passed in these also.

All Pass Fall Exams

Last spring, when the Michigan state bar examinations were given, 92 men entered. Of this number 42 passed, making the percentage 45.7. The fall examinations were given recently, and every Michigan man entered in the tests passed.

Authorities in the Law school are highly pleased with this showing as it bears out the confidence placed in this school by the leading law firms of the country, many of whom place requests with the dean every year for men to enter their offices. Figures from the Dean's office show that more requests for Michigan graduates were received last year than ever before and that the number has been steadily increasing.

BROOKLYN THROUGH WITH MARQUARD, SAYS EBBETTS

Cleveland, Oct. 12.—Pres. Charles Ebbetts of the Brooklyn National league club, tonight announced that Rube Marquard who was fined $1.00 and costs today for violating the exhibition ticket ordinance would never play with Brooklyn again.

"I'm through with him absolutely," said Mr. Ebbetts. "He hasn't been released, however, and if anybody else wants him, they can have him but Marquard will never again put on a Brooklyn uniform."

ADELPHI SOCIETY HAS FIRST MEETING OF YEAR

The Adelphi House of Representatives convened for the 11th session in Adelphi hall. George D. Wilner of the oratorical faculty spoke to the society on "The Man Who Does Make a Team."

Mr. Wilner was followed by short

POLISH-RUSS PACT SIGNED, ARMISTICE IN EFFECT 19TH

ANNOUNCEMENT BRINGS LARGE CROWDS TO PUBLIC SQUARE

TREATY OF GIVE AND TAKE BETWEEN NATIONS

Riga Settlement to Put Bolsheviki at Peace with All Their Baltic Neighbors

(By Associated Press)

Riga, Oct. 12.—A preliminary peace treaty and armistice was signed by the Polish and Russian soviet peace delegates at 7:10 o'clock tonight. The armistice actually becomes effective at midnight Oct. 18 or 144 hours from midnight tonight. The announcement that peace was to be signed brought great crowds to the public square.

About 200 persons, including the entire diplomatic body and prominent Lettish officials, crowded a small room, many of them standing.

Fear Treaty Will Not Satisfy

The head of the soviet delegation described the peace as "a peace without victory and without vanquished" in a brief address before the signing of the treaty. That describes the Riga agreement as it appeared to disinterested onlookers. It was a peace of give and take which followers fear will not be popular with either the Poles or the Soviet.

The Riga armistice will put the Bolsheviki at peace with all their Baltic neighbors and leave the Wrangle movement as the only great military operation remaining against the Soviets.

Nations Tired of War

M. Jompe called attention to the many difficulties encountered in arranging the armistice and also to the harmonious manner in which the delegations carried out the negotiations. He also expressed the belief that the foundation had been laid for a permanent peace, as both nations are absolutely tired of war and unwilling to assume the responsibility for continuing the struggle.

MAN-OF-WAR DEFEATS SIR BARTON 8 LENGTHS

AMERICAN JOCKEY SLOWS UP MOUNT IN LAST QUARTER

(By Associated Press)

Windsor, Oct. 12.—The thoroughbred championship of the continent tonight rests on the American side of the border. Man-of-War, the greatest three year old of years, galloped home with the honors at Kennilworth Jockey club this afternoon, a full eight lengths in front of Sir Barton, the great four year old from Commander J. K. L. Ross' stables. The time was 2:03, more than a full second faster than the old Canadian record for this distance.

Samuel D. Biddle of Philadelphia, owner of the victor, is the richer tonight by $75,000, the purse, and a gold cup valued at $5,000. The race was over a course of a mile and a quarter at weight for age, the winner carrying 120 pounds to the loser's 126. Between 29,000 and 30,000 persons paid to see the great horse race.

Sir Barton drew the pole and was away with a jump, but the lead was short lived. Jockey Kummer sent Man-of-War alongside and then ahead. When the stands were reached at the end of the first quarter, the Biddle horse had a two lengths lead. Kummer kept Man-of-War in check to the third quarter pole then let out a wrap, and the great three year old responded with a burst of speed that left Sir Barton eight lengths behind before the stretch was reached.

The last quarter mile around the stretch was an easy gallop with Kummer visibly easing up his mount.

DECLINES MOVIE OFFER TO WEAR FRESHMAN POT

Would you turn down a chance to make a trial picture for two prominent picture producing companies [illegible] picture published in the Motion Picture magazine [illegible] Film Fun? Really would you do all this just to come to Ann Arbor and wear a freshman pot?

Well, there is one man who did and he is Leo Nielzielski, one of the several thousands of yearlings who daily trot about the campus in quest of knowledge.

All of the above happened to Leo, yet he prefers to be a student at Michigan.

ROOM COMMITTEE FACES DIFFICULTY

Wholesale Exodus of Students from Contracted Rooms Causes Considerable Trouble

PRICES FALL SUDDENLY AS HOUSING SPACE INCREASES

Considerable difficulty is being experienced by the committee on appeal in connection with the housing situation because of a wholesale exodus within the last few days of students from contracted rooms.

The large number of rooms available in Ann Arbor at the present time has been the cause of a sudden lowering of room rents by landladies. In many cases students have moved out of contracted rooms, taking quarters at a much lower figure.

Complaints Received

Complaints have been received by the housing committee from irate landladies who are left with empty rooms, and the committee has taken a firm stand in regard to the situation.

No student may vacate, according to the committee, any room or suite of rooms contracted for, until the end of the semester, without first securing a tenant to take his place. In the event that an exorbitant figure is being charged for the rooms, the matter will be ironed out by the housing committee.

Troubles Settled

Few differences of the latter type have been brought to the attention of the committee, but in each case they have been settled to the satisfaction of both landlady and student-tenant.

The housing committee will be in session to hear all complaints from 2 to 3:30 o'clock Wednesday, Thursday, and Friday afternoons of this week in room 302 of the Union.

SOCIETY HEADS TO MEET WITH COOLEY

Dean Mortimer E. Cooley of the engineering college will meet with C. N. Johnston, '21E, president of the Engineering society, the four presidents of the different branches of the society, and the managing editor and business manager of the Technic, T. R. Gustafson, '21E, and W. R. Harrison, '21E, respectively, at 10 o'clock Saturday morning in his office.

The meeting is for the purpose of arranging the activties for the coming year to the plan of the new constitution of the Engineering society.

The society will hold meetings twice a month during the present year in order that the faculty and the students may be brought into closer contact with one another.

PROFESSOR SCOTT TO TELL OF EXPERIENCES IN EUROPE

Prof. Fred N. Scott of the Rhetoric department will be the speaker at the meeting of the Quadrangle society this evening. Taking as his subject "A Tale of Two Cities," Professor Scott will give the impressions he received while in England and France during

ARRANGEMENTS FOR INAUGURATION DAY ARE COMPLETED

DELEGATES AND OFFICIALS WILL BEGIN TO ARRIVE THIS EVENING

RECEPTION AND SMOKER TO BE GIVEN TONIGHT

Advance Copies of President's Speech Have Been Mailed to State and National Papers

With the selection of the line of march for the academic procession and designation of places of assembly for the units participating practically all the important arrangements were completed yesterday afternoon for the inauguration of President Marion L. Burton at 10:30 o'clock tomorrow morning.

Start from U. Hall

Forming in front of University hall, the procession will move along State street to North University avenue, to the library, then to Waterman gymnasium, and down North University avenue to Hill auditorium. There will be no procession in case of rain. A detailed statement as to places of assembly for those taking part in the procession is made this morning in The Daily Official Bulletin.

Students not holding tickets or the exercises will assemble at 8:30 o'clock south of the Engineering building on South University avenue.

Delegates and official guests will begin to arrive this evening, according to Prof. W. P. Lombard, chairman of the sub-committee on hospitality. All who have been registered are to be entertained at the homes of faculty members and citizens of Ann Arbor. Visiting university trustees and regents will be the guests of the University at the Michigan Union.

To Show Guests City

Auto service, under the direction of Prof. H. P. Thieme, will be provided, and guests will be met at the train and taken to the homes where they are to be entertained. Cars marked "Committee" will be on the streets at all times for the disposal of guests and their hosts. Drives through the city have been arranged for Thursday and Friday afternoons.

President Burton and Mrs. Burton will be at home informally tonight to delegates and guests, and the University club will give a smoker during the evening for the early arrivals.

University hall and other buildings are being decorated with American flags and the University colors, yellow and blue.

Mail Copies of Speeches

Advance copies of the address of President Burton on "The Function of the State University," were mailed last night to 650 papers in the state of Michigan by the committee on publicity, of which Prof. J. L. Brumm is chairman. Copies were also sent to 30 leading papers throughout the country. Abstracts of speeches to be delivered at the educational conference were sent out earlier.

Mrs. Booth Will Talk Here Monday

Mrs. Maude Ballington Booth, known as "the little mother of the prisons," will speak at 8 o'clock Monday evening in Hill auditorium under the auspices of the King's Daughters of the Congregational church. Mrs. Booth and her husband, the son of General Evangeline Booth, of the Salvation Army, founded the Volunteers of America.

The work of this organization is to re-establish released prisoners and to look after their families during the term of imprisonment. The prisoners have given Mrs. Booth her title in appreciation of her talks to them and the interest she has taken in their welfare. During the war she was overseas with the Y. M. C. A.

Mrs. Booth is an English woman, a

The Michigan Daily

ESTABLISHED 1890

EDITED AND MANAGED BY THE STUDENTS OF THE UNIVERSITY OF MICHIGAN

MEMBER ASSOCIATED PRESS

VOL. XLI, NO. 2 — TWELVE PAGES — ANN ARBOR, MICHIGAN, TUESDAY, SEPTEMBER 30, 1930 — TWO SECTIONS — PRICE FIVE CENTS

ENROLLMENT IN UNIVERSITY SHOWS 648 DECREASE

NEW FACULTY MEN ASSUME POSITIONS AS SESSION BEGINS

Additional Instructors in Many Departments Commence Teaching Duties.

McKENZIE TO GET POST

Besekirsky, Hackett, Brinkman, Littlefield, Doty Added to Music Staff.

With the beginning of the 1930-31 school year yesterday a large number of new members of the faculty assumed their duties in connection with the teaching staff of the University. Several of them are men especially well-known in their various fields of work.

In the English department, Prof. Howard Mumford Jones, noted as an author, poet, critic, and teacher, has been added to the staff. Formerly of North Carolina, his special interest has been in the study of the French influence in early American literature.

Prof. Vernor W. Crane has been appointed professor of American history. He comes to Michigan after 14 years on the faculty of Brown university where he was especially known for his work in the history of the period of the American revolution. He studied at Michigan under the late Prof. Claude H. Van Tyne and will direct the courses which were formerly taught by Professor Van Tyne.

McKenzie to Teach.

As head of the department of sociology, a position left vacant by the death of Prof. Charles H. Cooley last year, Prof. Robert D. McKenzie will come to Michigan at the beginning of the second semester. He has been associated with the University of Washington and at the present time, is carrying on initial welfare work in Chicago.

Prof. John E. Tracy, formerly of Chicago and one of the leading corporation experts in the country, has joined the faculty of the Law school. He will give a course of lectures in "Corporation Practice."

To Head Observatory.

Prof. Heber D. Curtis, a member of the faculty of the University of Pittsburgh since 1920 and of the staff of the Allegheny observatory of the University of Pittsburgh since 1902, will be professor of astronomy and director of the University observatory.

Wassily Besekirsky, professor of violin and noted violinist, and Arthur Hackett, professor of voice, have joined the staff of the Music school faculty as heads of their respective departments. Other new members of the faculty include Hanns Pick, Joseph Brinkman, instructor of piano, and William Doty, instructor in organ.

Botany Faculty Increased.

New members of the Botany department faculty are Prof. Edwin A. Evans, professor of botany and acting director of the University arboretum, who comes from Purdue, and Prof. William R. Taylor who comes here from the University of Pennsylvania as assistant professor of botany and curator of algae for the University herbarium.

In addition to Professor Crane's appointment to the faculty of the history department is the appointment of Dwight Dumond as assistant professor of American history. His special interest is southern and ante-bellum American history. He has his Ph.D. from Michigan. William Landers and M. Kempers are his instructors in history.

In the romance languages department, Camilo B. Bejino comes from Bryn Mawr as instructor of Italian while there. Two courses, one in Italian. Jacques J. (Continued on Page 2.)

CLUB OFFER WILL CLOSE TOMORROW

Time is Extended for Special Subscription Rate.

Although originally planned to hold only during Orientation week, the Students' Publications Club subscription offer will be continued until 5 o'clock Wednesday afternoon due to the large demand for the club rates.

This club subscription offer includes a year's subscription to The Daily, Michigan's student newspaper which carries complete news of the campus in addition to special features, editorials, and official University announcements. All news of national and international interest is obtained through special arrangement with the Associated Press.

In addition, this offer includes a year's subscription to the Gargoyle, Michigan's monthly humor magazine and one dollar's credit towards the purchase of a Michiganensian, year-book of the University.

AUTO BAN REMAINS STRICT, SAYS REA

Rigid Enforcement of Previous Regulations Will Continue Effective This Year.

TO LIST STORED CARS

Registration of all cars stored by students during their residence in Ann Arbor and an unyielding enforcement of the auto ban were announced by Walter B. Rea, assistant to the dean of students, this morning with the opening of the 1930-31 enforcement period. Rea stated that regulations governing the auto ban would remain the same this year as they have in previous terms.

For students entering the University for the first time, Rea suggested that the rule be read carefully as published in numerous freshman publications at the beginning of the present school year.

Briefly the rule stated that no student may operate a motor vehicle during the official school year with the exception of definitely stated times preceding and following vacation periods when the ban is temporarily lifted. This rule passed by the Board of Regents in 1927, has never been seriously modified though between 250 and 500 permits are issued every year to students finding automobiles necessary for business purposes only. Ann Arbor students are also given family privileges through University permits, although personal and social use of cars by Michigan students is strictly forbidden in any case.

Violation of the auto ban is punishable by expulsion from the University or probation for a long period according to the offense and the circumstances governing it, Dean Rea explained.

Professional students or students living in Ann Arbor with their wives who find it necessary for business purposes to drive cars are given permits under the more liberal interpretation of the auto ban ruling, Rea pointed out.

Cars stored in Ann Arbor by students from points long distant from the University must be registered with license number and location of garage in the office of the assistant to the dean.

LOOTING ATTENDS WEEK-END GAMES

Police records yesterday were filled with the customary total of petty robbery reports which always accompany a football week-end in Ann Arbor.

Four automobiles were reported stolen Saturday and one home was looted by burglars, according to local police records. Cars owned by

LATEST RECOUNT GIVES GROESBECK SLIGHT INCREASE

Check-Up, Nearly Done, Shows Gain of 100 Ballots for Former Governor.

NET OF 2,400 CLAIMED

Further Re-Checking of Several Hundred Precincts Started to End Dispute.

(By Associated Press)

LANSING, Sept. 29.—One recount of the votes cast in the Republican gubernatorial primary was practically completed today. Another, which will cover several hundred precincts, immediately got under way. The latter already is closed to controversy.

Further court action was indicated several times by counsel for Alex J. Groesbeck. They said a ruling by the Supreme court Saturday established their rights and hinted they may again go to court if they deem it necessary.

When the day's activities ended, the official tabulation for the original recount, with only scattering precincts missing, showed Groesbeck had made a net gain 100 votes or less.

Barnard Protests.

Three auditors were moved into the recount chamber by Groesbeck's forces, and they claimed the former governor's net is around 2,400. The wide divergence of figures brought Everett A. Barnard, attorney for Groesbeck to protest to the State Board of Canvassers that "the recount is in such a muddle no one knows where either Groesbeck or Wilbur M. Brucker stand." He demanded a complete second count of all precincts, and a completely new system of tabulation. The State board denied his request, ruling that only such precincts as were ordered recounted by the State Supreme Court will be checked a second time.

COUNCIL TO MEET WEDNESDAY NIGHT

Election of Two Juniors to Fill Vacancies Will be Held.

Election of two juniors to fill the vacancies in the Student Council, is expected to feature the first meeting of the undergraduate governing body tomorrow night. Appointment of committee chairmen and selection of the officers of the council will also be in order at the meeting.

The vacancies caused by the scholastic ineligibility of John D. Hubley '32, and by the absence of Thomas G. Roach '32, from the University this year, will be filled through choice by the council as a whole. Because of the amendment to the constitution last year providing that the membership be of 15 members with the election of two additional juniors? That council this year will be larger than in the past.

It is expected that the council will also discuss and decide on the dates for the parties of the four classes. Since both the Sophomore Prom and the Frosh Frolic have lost money the past few years, the idea of uniting the two will be considered.

2100 NEWCOMERS MEET IN ANNUAL FRESHMAN WEEK

Mathematics, Rhetoric, English Psychology Tests Greet Class of 1934.

350 ADVISERS ATTEND

Orientation Period Featured by Address of Laurence Gould, Assistant to Byrd.

Freshmen donned their pots yesterday for the first time with the opening of the 1930-31 term of school following one of the most successful Orientation week programs in the history of Michigan Prof. Philip A. Bursley, in charge of the entire week's program stated that in order to carry out the year's initial effort on incoming students a corps of more than 350 advisers, both from the faculty and student body, were necessary.

A total of approximately 2,100 entering the University for the first time were put through their paces by the advising staff which averaged one for every eight students. Of this number 1350 were freshmen entering Michigan without advanced credit, 750 were transfers from other colleges and universities, and a few returning to Michigan after absences of several years.

Special Staffs Assist

Along with the crew of 350 advisers, a staff of 40 members in the library and between 50 and 60 medical students at Waterman gymnasium assisted in the processing of entering freshmen and upperclassmen. Several members of the Intramural staff were engaged throughout the week on tours of the building.

The week's program was carried on in exactly the scheduled manner. Every event on the program was run off within a few minutes of the time scheduled.

Covered Shortened Period

Between 1,900 and 2,000 students were given medical examination during the first week. Of this number a great percentage were freshmen, all of whom were subjected to rigid physical tests. Mental examinations were given to all entering freshmen in psychology, mathematics, rhetoric and English.

Features of the week aside from the usual mass sing, lectures, pre-professional conferences, and welcoming addresses included a talk by Dr. Laurence M. Gould, famous geologist with the recent Byrd expedition, and the fact that but four and a half days were used in comparison to the six of previous years.

Mendelssohn Theatre Will Present Dancer

Carola Goya, Spanish dancer, will present the local season's first dancing recital at the Lydia Mendelssohn theatre, according to an announcement made yesterday by Amy Loomis, director. She will appear at 8:30 o'clock, Saturday, October 4.

"Carola Goya," stated Miss Loomis, "was an outstanding success in New York last season, where she gave 18 recitals. She is famous because her dances are authentic. She lived last year in the mountains in Spain, getting real Spanish folk dances, which will be on the program Saturday night."

BOOKLET REVIEWS COMING LECTURES

Byrd's Talk to Open Oratorical Association Series.

Henry Moser of the speech department, business manager of the Oratorical association, announced yesterday the publication of a booklet containing a review of the speakers who will appear on the program of the Association's series this year.

First on the list is Rear-Admiral Richard E. Byrd, who will talk on "Flying to the South Pole" on November 10 in Hill auditorium.

Third on the program is William Hard, noted Washington newspaper man, who will talk on "What Makes Politicians that Way?" He will appear on December

PLANS SCHEDULE FOR BROADCASTS

Prof. Waldo M. Abbot.

Director of University broadcasting, who has announced the completion of plans for the programs to be presented this year over station WJR, Detroit.

ABBOT ANNOUNCES BROADCAST PLANS

Radio University to Commence Programs. Michigan Night Will Be Continued.

HOBBS, KIPKE TO SPEAK

University of Michigan radio programs which are broadcast through the facilities of station WJR, Detroit will be divided into three groups for the current University year, according to Prof. Waldo Abbot, director of radio broadcasting. Every Sunday afternoon from 5 to 5:30 o'clock the Parents' Program will be put on the air addressed primarily to the Parent-Teachers associations of Michigan. The popular University program which is being broadcast for the sixth year will be heard from 7:30 to 8:30 o'clock. The Michigan University of the Air programs will be of half-hour duration, starting at 2 o'clock every Monday, Tuesday, Wednesday, and Thursday.

The Parent programs while addressed primarily to the Parent-Teacher Associations are planned to be of universal interest to those interested in parental education, according to Professor Abbot. These programs will contain one talk approximately 12 minutes in duration, and the balance of the period will be devoted to music. The soloist for the opening program will be Frank Ryan of Ann Arbor, graduate student of the University School of Music.

The opening Michigan night program on October 4 will present only two speakers, Harry Kipke, (Continued on Page 2.)

Literary College Losses Exceed 500 in Early Estimates

Unofficial Figures Point to Marked Slump in Number Enrolled in University for Current Semester.

LAW FINDS SILENCER MUFFLES ITS OWNER

MARQUETTE, Mich, Sept 29—The state police had a little too fast for Marcus Roberts today. Weeks ago Roberts ordered a rifle silencer from Europe. It arrived today at his home in Northland. But just at the same time, the state police arrived also, and after unpacking the silencer for Roberts, arrested him for having it in his possession.

KNOPF WILL OPEN UNIVERSITY SERIES

Fourteen Speakers Scheduled for Appearances During Lecture Season.

LEVI-BRUHL WILL TALK

Prominent speakers and scholars from many countries will appear here during the coming season on the lecture series sponsored by the University announced yesterday.

Outstanding among those already engaged is Hjalmar Schacht, former president of the Reichsbank in Germany. Another lecturer of note who will address University audiences is Prof. Levi-Bruhl, of the University of Paris. Professor Levi-Bruhl is an eminent sociologist, and was invited here by the sociology department of the University.

Others in the series include Prof. Weinberg of the Institute Pasteur, Prof. Edward Kramers of the University of Wisconsin, mineralogist; Prof. Gilson, a French philosopher; Gerhardt von Chulze Gavernitz, Fribourg, Germany, economist; Prof. Franz Knopf and S.P.L. Sorenson, physiological chemists; W. E. Hiley, who will speak on forestry.

Prof. Vladimir Ipartieff, who has been invited by Prof. Moses Gombers; the well known naturalist and Australian official Melbourne Ward, Henry A. Pilsby, curator of mollusks at the Philadelphia Academy of Natural Sciences, and Martin Sprengling of the Semitics department of the University of Chicago. Two of the lecturers are well known on this campus, Dr. Sylvanus G. Morley official of the (Continued on Page 2.)

REGENTS CONVENE IN FIRST MEETING

Separation of Aeronautics from Marine Department Made.

At the meeting of the Regents at regular meeting held last Friday will make the division of aeronautical engineering, which since it was founded in 1916, has been under the jurisdiction of the department of marine engineering. Ralph H. Upson of Detroit, an authority on aeronautics, was appointed to act as lecturer on lighter-than-air aircraft, and Felix W. Pawlowski, a member of the engineering school, was appointed to a similar position on heavier-than-air craft. Herbert C. Sadler, dean of the engineering school, was reappointed to head the new department.

Announcement was made of a gift of $5,000 from B. Eberhardt of Ann Arbor and will permit Prof. Leroy Waterman of the Semitics department

The College of Literature Science and the Arts shows a marked falling off. From 4584 the total at this time last year to 4030, a loss of 554. In the college 2602 of the number enrolled are men while 1428 are women.

Engineers Lose 15.

The Colleges of Engineering and Architecture show a slight decrease of 15, or 15 students less than last year. The medical school has decreased in size from 631 to 545. Men in this school number 500 and women 45. The Law school which dropped from 568 to 502 has 43 women enrolled.

The Pharmacy college which has 78 men and eight women shows an increase of four students over the number enrolled at this time last year. The School of Dentistry, however, dropped from 324 students to 278, or 46 less than last year. The total number enrolled in the Graduate school is 630 with 283 of that number being women. In the School of Education the students number 360 with 246 of the number being women and 114 men. The School of Business Administration has an enrollment of 109.

Rumors Found Groundless

Forty-one men are registered in the School of Forestry and Conservation, and the music school has a total enrollment of 186 of which 55 are men and 131 women.

Numerous false reports have been circulating concerning the enrollment in the freshman class, according to officials in the office of the registrar. These reports which state that the number of freshman women in the University exceeds the number of men is false as is shown by figures on freshman registration. These figures are not as yet complete, however, it is understood that the number is less than that of last year.

CHORAL SOCIETY PLANS TRYOUTS

Prof. Earl V. Moore, of the music school, announced dates for the Choral Union tryouts yesterday. Tryouts will be asked to report in room 107 of the music school from 5 to 9 o'clock on Tuesday on Wednesday, 1 to 5

FRESHMEN MEET HAZY RECEPTION AT OPENING OF COLLEGE CAREERS

Pots, hesitantly worn adjacent to outstanding left ears, unaccountably aroused the wrath of certain deep thinkers yesterday. Freshmen, sometimes belligerent but more often meek, carried books and packages

An unwonted chivalry was apparent among the first year men. Many were seen to conduct women across the streets through heavy traffic, while others obligingly

1930

The 1930 cover of *The Michigan Daily* introduces the paper's first headline* that is extra bold and spans accross the whole page, all seven columns. As you may notice, the paper is even larger, adding yet another column since 1920. With the exception of a single vertical photograph in a small portion of one column, the cover is still completely reliant on textual elements. While we have seen rules dividing stories horizontally within a column, this is also the first time that columns are merged together. If you look to the top of the two far right columns, you will see one headline taking up two column widths, without a line dividing the columns. This is the first real experimentation with the grid, and marks a transition from purely vertical formats to more geometric story formats.

* A heading at the top of an article or page in a newspaper or magazine.

1940

The greatest change in *The Michigan Daily*'s 1940 cover is the consistent font selection for all headlines. Instead of alternating between consensed sans serifs and serifs, and italics and size, the headlines stick to one, bold serif font. This unifies the stories and creates a more cohesive visual identity. While this adjustment is an improvement from 1930, the other elements of the grid are also less daring. There is no bold headline that stretches accross all seven columns, and the column number and width remain the same. One picture does take up two columns, as does the headline that goes with it, but beyond that they do not push the limits of the seven column, vertical grid.

Weather
[...]udy, somewhat colder
[...]ith occasional snow.

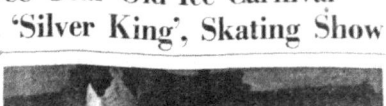

The Michigan Daily

Editorial
[illegible]

No. 101 Z-223 ANN ARBOR, MICHIGAN, THURSDAY, FEB. 22, 1940 PRICE FIVE CENTS

[...]ssia Orders [...]ne Experts [...]m Turkish [...]ustry Posts

[...]n Calls For Exodus [...] Technicians After [...]t German Move; Talks Of War

[...]UL, Feb. 21.—(AP)—Soviet [...]y called home hundreds [...] technical experts em[...] years in Turkish industry [...]ssian-Turkish agreement. [...]odus will follow closely [...]chnicians from Germany. [...]rtner. Russia already was [...]her commercial organiza[...]s country and Germany. [...]orld War ally is doing

[...]ssians ordered by the [...] leave immediately, were [...] embark with their fami[...]ssa. Russian Black Sea [...]Russian Embassy at An[...]eived the order and then [...]e affected.

[...]key Is Worried

[...] action came at a time [...]rkish press openly is dis[...]possibility of war in this [...]world in the spring, per[...]nious about Russia's rich [...]he Caucasus just across [...]border.

[...] Ismet Inonu and the [...]eral staff recently in[...] Russian frontier and [...]ed to survey the Greek [...]n border fortifications.

[...]iable quarters reported [...] British engineer offi[...]ved at Adrianople [...]rtifications on the Bul[...]r, where work recently [...] by the army.

War Footing

[...]ally of Great Britain [...]t so far a non-belliger[...]y on a war footing and [...]ng to her fortifications [...]s well to her domestic

[...]o the Turkish press [...]ter the war the mom[...]n power attacks the [...]nse military prepara[...]ation with Britain and [...] been under way for [...]s strategic region, key [...]ack door."

[...]Of 1940 [...]llect Dues

[...] To Be Solicited [...]ach Member

[...]f one dollar per stu[...]ected by the Finance [...]e Class of 1940 start[...]y in Angell Hall, it [...] last night by Mar[...], treasurer.

[...] purpose of the dues [...]llows:

[...] senior class page in

[...]idental expenditures [...]nd stationery.

[...] a fund which will be [...] the Class Officers' [...]Alumni Association. [...]e used to keep class [...]ther after gradua[...]ning contacts be[...]d members and pro[...]s at five-year in[...]

[...]mmittee consists of [...]nan, Wally Hinkle, [...] Crossman, Miriam [...]t, Ruth Chapard, [...]ordon Laing and [...]e also on the com[...]

[...]t Hiccuping [...]at (Hic) Is?

[...]'43, has been tak[...]g on his head, [...]hile plugging his [...]g accusations of [...] hours now, but his [...]gn of stopping. [...]tent affliction, [...]ary defines as a [...] inspiratory move[...]esday afternoon. [...] said last night in [...]mingled with ex[...]ceen able to stop [...]

Dorm Workers Protest Heard By University

Certain "suggestions" made by University dormitory workers will be "taken under consideration" during the next few days by University officials, it was announced yesterday following a conference between Vice-President Shirley W. Smith and representatives of an AFL union of dormitory workers.

The conference had been requested by members of the union, who claimed that wage rates and working conditions were below adequate standards.

Vice-President Smith announced after the meeting that he had heard "certain definite requests," and said that the University would "take them under consideration."

Mr. Smith said that a "clear promise" had been made to the workers that dormitory officials would not "discriminate" in any manner against employees who joined the Union.

Representatives of the labor union announced that the meeting had been "successful from every standpoint," and said that they expected to meet with University officials sometime early in March.

Among the "suggestions" which were made at the meeting, the labor leaders said, were proposals for "better wages, better working conditions, better overtime wages, and improved regulations in general."

Egyptian Curse Branded False By Steindorff

University Lecturer Says Articles About Tombs Are 'Merely Stories'

A scientist who has outlived the men of his generation, Dr. Georg Steindorff, famed Egyptologist and former professor in the University of Leipzig, came to Ann Arbor yesterday to present his views on peoples of ancient Egypt.

Aged Dr. Steindorff, who is one of the founders of the modern study of Egyptology, discredited the popular belief that an ancient curse falls upon present-day defilers of Egyptian tombs.

In an interview following his lecture in Rackham Amphitheatre, Dr. Steindorff branded the numerous newspaper articles about the supposed curse as "merely stories." He explained that only one curse against the opening of tombs existed, and applied in the distant past to the Egyptian practice of reutilizing crypt stones for building purposes.

The unfortunate deaths which have been attributed to the King Tutankhamen excavations were obviously caused by natural forces, he asserted, the last death taking place 15 years after the tomb's discovery.

Michigan's Three Year Old Ice Carnival Will Present 'Silver King', Skating Show

A three year-old campus baby which makes a shivering appearance each winter will let out a lusty bellow at 8 p.m. tomorrow in the Coliseum and then slap its royal rattle on the noggin of a local big-wig.

The moniker of the gurgling infant is the University of Michigan Ice Carnival. The cranium to be crowned tomorrow night by the tot's celluloid scepter is that of Footballist Forest Evashevski '41, henceforth to be designated the Carnival's "Silver King."

Two developments yesterday marked the extensive preparations for the frozen-water frolic. They were:

1. An air-mail cargo of "treasure" to be distributed by the Silver King during the evening was shipped from New York City, the only place where such treasure can be found.

No Jitterbugs

2. Local long-hairs clapped a ban on rug-cutting after the regular program, as had been announced. Objections were raised by the rink managers, in a stirring condemnation of jitterbugging, jiving and hep-cats.

Earlier, the program for the Ice Carnival had been announced by relays of public relations counsellors. Leading the show will be the Detroit Olympia Skating Club and its stars, Erice Jaddec and Evelyn Denne, as solo events. Robert Gach, Arcade shutter-snapper, may burlesque the antics of a bewildered photographer who attempted to cover last year's Carnival. Others on runners will be two skaters from Michigan State College and Mary Francis Greschke and Betty Courtwright, Ann Arbor figure skating champions.

Free Skating From 9:30-11 P.M.

The free-skating session will last from 9:30 to 11 p.m., having been lengthened because of the dancing ban.

Final entries were announced for the fraternity and sorority skating relays to be held as part of the program. Sororities entering are: Alpha Gamma Delta, Alpha Omicron Pi, Chi Omega, Collegiate Sorosis, Delta Gamma, Gamma Phi Beta, and Delta Delta Delta. Fraternity teams are: Sigma Alpha Epsilon, Phi Kappa Psi, Phi Psi, Chi Psi, Delta Upsilon and Sigma Phi Epsilon.

Included in the program to be given by the Olympia Club are group and solo numbers. Solos and pairs by Miss Greschke and Miss Courtwright will also be presented as will waltzes featuring ice figures.

— Photo by Merriman.

Hairy-armed Forest Evashevski, football captain and a all-around muscle man, is the successor to Michigan's carnival queen, officials of the University ice carnival announced today. Evashevski will be a "Silver King." Shown with him in the picture above is Mary Francis Greschke, Ann Arbor figure skater.

Tryouts For Spanish Play Will Be Conducted Friday

Final tryouts for the annual Spanish play, "Zaragueta," a "comedy of customs" by Ramos Carrion and Vital Aza, will be held at 3 p.m. tomorrow in Room 312 Romance Language Building.

Seven men and four women are needed for the play, which will be held April 1. Any student is eligible to try out, even though he is not studying Spanish at the present time, according to Dr. Charles Staubach, director of the play.

'Unofficial Editor' Tom Patterson Resigns His Position With Daily

By STAN SWINTON

When youthful newspapermen return to visit their alma mater, point No. 1 on their itinerary is a trip to the Student Publications Building and Tom Patterson.

They come back to see the tall, handsome typesetter because in his five years with The Michigan Daily he has proved himself the amateur journalists' best friend. When headlines didn't count and the fast-approaching deadline proved too much for the night editor's composure, it was Tom Patterson who saved the situation by writing the headline on the linotype without outside help. When a late story was rushed in seconds before the paper was due to go to press, it was Tom Patterson's nimble finger which performed the seemingly impossible and had the story ready in time.

That's all over now. Last night Tom Patterson announced he had resigned his position with The Daily to become vice-president and general manager of the Patterson Brothers printing firm.

"There's one last thing I'd like to do for the boys, though," Tom said as he leaned back in his typesetter's chair. "So tell 'em there'll be a keg of beer waiting Friday afternoon."

"You know," he continued, [...]

TOM PATTERSON

Mich. and a dozen other towns. Throughout the mid-west and west he is famed in printing circles as one of the fastest typesetters and best [...]

Catholic View Will Be Heard In Faith Series

Washington's Rev. Furfey Will Give Second SRA Lecture Saturday Night

Presenting the orthodox Catholic viewpoint on the "Existence and Nature of Religion," The Rev. Paul H. Furfey, professor of sociology at the Catholic University, Washington, D.C. will deliver the second lecture in the current Student Religious Association series on religion at 8 p.m. Saturday in the Rackham Lecture Hall.

Delivering the belief of the Catholic who is both scientist and clergyman, Father Furfey is one of four noted speakers who are being brought to the Campus by the SRA to discuss the different viewpoints they hold on the question of religion.

Father Furfey, who is a Fellow of the American Association for the Advancement of Science and co-director of the Catholic University's Center for Research in Child Development, has been supplied with a copy of Prof. Anton J. Carlson's lecture, which was delivered here last Friday and which attacked religion on the grounds of science. It is expected that his lecture will, in part, deal with Professor Carlson's stand.

Ruthven's Ten Years Honored

New York Alumni To Fete President At Banquet

President Ruthven's 10 years of service as president of the University will be celebrated tomorrow night at the Annual Banquet of the University of Michigan Club of New York, to be held in the Waldorf-Astoria Hotel. Dr. Ruthven himself will be the guest of honor.

Representing the University and giving short toasts to Michigan will be Regent Edmund C. Shields, Shirley W. Smith, vice-president and secre[...]

Michigan Team Swims Against Gophers Today

Wolverines Have Enough Strength To Take First Place In Every Event

By DON WIRTCHAFTER

Minnesota's mermen are prepared for the worst today, for they are playing hosts to the Michigan superman swimming team in the Gopher tank tonight.

Fresh from a record-smashing 70-14 triumph over Michigan State, Matt Mann has brought 14 of his Western Conference and National Collegiate champions to Minneapolis to extend Michigan's dual meet win streak to seven.

To say that Minnesota doesn't stand a chance tonight is putting it mildly. The Wolverines, with the strongest array of talent in Michigan history, can and will win as they please.

Even with a record of four wins against two setbacks, Neils Thorpe's aggregation can't be considered a threat to Matt Mann's unblemished record. While Michigan trampled over Iowa, 63-21, the Gopher mermen fell before the same Hawkeye attack, 56-28.

Mann left two of his aces at home, but it won't change the complexion of tonight's affair. Even with Bill Beebe and Strother "T-Bone" Martin out of the Michigan lineup, the Wolverines still have enough power to win every event.

In the diving, Mann has Capt. Hal

(Continued on Page 3)

Finnish Dancers To Be Featured At Relief Concert

Finnish folk dancers wearing authentic costumes of Finland will appear in the program of the campus Finnish relief concert to be given Tuesday in Hill Auditorium, Toivo [...]

All 'A' Students Are Announced In Four Schools

Announcement of students who received all "A" records in the engineering college, the school of business administration, the pharmacy school and the graduate school was made by University officials yesterday.

Graduate School

Students who received perfect records were:

Harold F. Allen, Henry N. Berhas, Jack Bookstein, Jean Brown, K. H. Chao, Irving M. Copilowish, Morris Dansky, Joshua Domashevitsky, Kenneth Evashevski, Lawrence J. Giacoletto, Harold M. Hefman, Robert Herzog, George L. Hill.

Frederick M. Hoblit, Howard S. Hoyman, Ingeborg V. Kayko, Wm. L. Kilhoine, Arthur Klein, Chas. A. Ormsby, Chas. E. Rickart, Frank G. Ryder, Fannie L. Shisler, Jean P. Slater, Henry S. Smith, Taft Y. Toribara, Donald J. Vink, Bernard Vinegrade, Clyde Vroman, Max A. Woodbury, Sherman A. Hoslett.

College of Engineering

Robert R. Allen, Charles B. Armstrong, Claude O. Broders, Don B. Carson, Jarrett R. Clark, James M. Eastman, Frank J. Feely, Jr., Edward A. Gaugler, Allen F. Gilliard, Herbert D. Hamilton.

Lewis O. Heinze, Harper H. Hull, Herbert L. Misch, Kenneth M. Nelson, Carl J. Oxford, Earl Schaefer, Bernard Shacter, Cornelius R. Skutt, Frederick B. Sleator, Lewis F. Smith, Charles M. Thatcher, Robert T. Wallace.

Business Administration

Elizabeth Helen Christen, Elinore Evelyn Clark, Douglas A. Hayes.

Pharmacy

William Lee Austin.

1,400 Persons See Benedict's Science Show

Demonstration Of Magic Thrills Large Audience In Rackham Auditorium

More than 1,400 students, faculty and townspeople yesterday heard and saw Dr. Francis G. Benedict's combination lecture and magic show in Rackham picture hall.

Before his demonstration Dr. Benedict contended that there is a basis for a comparison between science and magic. He said "that magic has shown you truth is much farther from being obvious than you believe."

In proving his contention, Dr. Benedict utilized the scientifically impossible technique of regeneration. After cutting a dollar bill diagonally with his so-called magic scissors and marking the serial number on a big white card, he asked two audience representatives to burn it. Handcuffing himself to these two students, he rubbed the ashes deliberatley, and methodically drew out the same dollar bill burned only a few seconds before.

Talking of the magician in the lecture which was entitled "Science and the Magician," Dr. Benedict pointed out that mystification of the audience might be accomplished by a trick, illusion or magical effect. Trick, he defined as "purely a mechanical or digital procedure involving skill." An illusion, he said, is "a glorified trick made possible by paraphernalia." As for magical effects, which are the highest art of the magician, he said they are "procedures demonstrating seeming violations of natural laws."

Crandall Picks Debate Squad

Eight Women To Compete In Contests This Year

Eight women who will participate in inter-collegiate women's debate this semester were named yesterday by Mrs. Frederic O. Crandall, women's debate coach.

The negative team which will make the trip to Purdue University March 12 will consist of Barbara Newton, '41, and Janet Grace, '42. The two teams which will meet University of Indiana squads here March 14 and Elizabeth Lightner, '41, and Jane Krause, '41, on the affirmative and [...]

Swedish Town Is Bombarded During Soviet Airplane Raid

Scandinavia Has Worries As Result Of Violation Of Swedish Neutrality; No Casualties Reported

STOCKHOLM, Feb. 21.—(AP)—Swooping Russian planes today bombed and fired the little Swedish border town of Pajala in an incident that threatened to rekindle the fiery Swedish movement for intervention in Finland.

Although all of Pajala's 2,000 residents escaped death, and the shower of 134 bombs was believed aimed at Finnish territory just six miles away, neutral observers expressed the opinion that Swedish "activists" now would reopen their drive to help Finland "so vigorously that other help is unnecessary."

34 Bombs Explosive

Townspeople estimated that 34 of the bombs from the heavily laden raiders were explosive, the remaining 100 incendiary. The fact that there were no casualties was credited to a timely warning flashed from the border and by the heroic work of a girl telephone operator who stuck at her post.

Most of the fell about was dropped in the center of town.

Among the demolished buildings were an apartment house and a saw mill from which workers just had time to flee. Bombs rained about a church in which terrorized townsfolk had huddled, shattering many of its windows.

Bombers Fly Low

The weather was clear and the bombers flew as low as 3,000 feet.

The Swedish government ordered its envoy to Moscow, Vilhelm Assarsson, to make an immediate and vigorous protest at the Kremlin.

Weight was added to the theory that there would be a resurgence of the "activist" movement by the ch[...] of the Swedish Finland commit[...] just back from Finland. He s[...] nounced tonight that an agree[...] had been reached with Finla[...] whereby the Swedish commit[...] would intensify the recruiting [...] Swedish volunteers.

Girl Is Hurt In Auto Cras[...]

Three Car Accident Resu[...] In Injury Of Detroite[...]

Miss Alice Pettibone, 16 years [...] was seriously injured last night [...] freak three car accident at the c[...] of Geddes and Forest while ridin[...] a car driven by Mrs. Dena V. Bre[...] 26, wife of Warren E. Brezette, [...] Ed.

Miss Pettibone suffered a deep [...] across her face requiring num[...] stitches and lacerations about [...] skull. University Hospital off[...] said last night that her skull wa[...] fractured. Mrs. Brezette was no[...] iously injured.

The accident occurred when [...] Brezette's car, travelling wes[...] Geddes, collided with a car driv[...] Sylvester Eldridge, 35, Negro, [...] was going north on Forest. The[...] mobiles careened up on to the [...] walk on Forest and turned bac[...] the street, ramming a parked c[...] longing to Norman Van Cor o[...] York City. The parked car wa[...] slightly damaged, but the oth[...] were demolished.

Miss Pettibone, from Detroi[...] been living with the Brezettes [...] city at 2014 Geddes. Eldridge [...] at 602 Gott. Eldridge was unin[...] according to officials at St. Jo[...] Hospital.

SRA Inaugurates [...] Oriental Semi[...]

Outlining the philosophy a[...] toms of Hinduism, Mrs. Fr[...] Thivy, [...]uate student f[...] dia, in[...]d the first of [...] of semi[...] Oriental Re[...] sponso[...]he Student R[...] Association, last night at La[...]

Designed to furnish info[...] which is not provided by Un[...] courses in religions, the sem[...]

25

MICHIGAN SPIRIT
See Page 4

The Michigan Daily

Latest Deadline in the State

CLOUDY

LXI, No. 4 · ANN ARBOR, MICHIGAN FRIDAY, SEPTEMBER 29, 1950 · EIGHT PAGES

MacArthur Parades as Korean Reds Flee

.S. Outlines Proposal for Free Korea

Denies Wish for Military Bases

NEW YORK—(AP)—A six-point United States program for creating a free and united Korea under the guidance of the whole United Nations was outlined by American spokesmen at the UN yesterday.

The Americans disclaimed any wish for military bases in Korea and called for urgent steps to rehabilitate the war-torn land.

THE AMERICAN program, which dovetails closely with a proposal being circulated by the British, follows in brief:

1. Korea should be free and united.

2. The method of unification can be determined by a strong United Nations commission in Korea with between seven and fourteen members.

3. **Korean people to be consulted by the commission should be chosen in free elections by secret ballot on the basis of universal suffrage.**

4. Strong emphasis on a program of rehabilitation and reconstruction.

5. **Settlement of the Korean problem must not be dominated by any one nation but must be accomplished by the United Nations in cooperation with the Korean people.**

6. It must be made certain that a free and independent Korea will be no threat to its neighbors.

Booth To Sell Football Ducat

A booth for the resale of surplus tickets to the Michigan State game will be open in the Union lobby from 9 p.m. till noon tomorrow, according to Charles Re..n, Union Councilman.

Persons wishing to sell extra tickets may leave them at the booth tomorrow, where they will be sold at regular prices. No student tickets may be resold, Re..n said.

Students who failed to pick up their tickets according to their group schedules will have their final chance from 8:30 to 4:30 Monday and Tuesday in the Athletic Administration Office at Ferry Field, Don Weir, ticket manager, announced.

Additional tickets may still be purchased for all home games except the Michigan State game, which has been completely sold out, according to Weir.

All the remaining seats are for end zone locations. Box seat tickets are still available for all other home games except Illinois and Northwestern, Weir said.

Rushing Deadline

Last chance for men to register for fraternity rushing will be from ... to 5 p.m. today and 9 a.m. to noon tomorrow in Rm. 3D of the Union, according to Bruce Sodee, ... Interfraternity Council rushing chairman.

A $2 fee is charged for registration. Rushing will begin with open houses Sunday afternoon and Monday night.

Coed Hospitalized

An 18-year-old University coed was taken to University Hospital by Ann Arbor police yesterday after she suddenly broke into a fit of screaming in front of Angell Hall.

Gov. Williams Proclaims 'Atom Day'

'A-Day' Proclamation

The following is Gov. William's Atom Day proclamation:

Forces which throughout time will affect the lives of all mankind have been set in motion by the release of atomic energy.

If these forces are to build rather than destroy, they must be identified and controlled. The sooner we learn to live with the atom, the sooner will we benefit by the now incredible potentialities of atomic science.

In these days of world-wide ideological conflict, the United States and its free people must take the lead in applying the awe-inspiring possibilities of atomic science to the promotion of universal health and welfare. The University of Michigan is now engaged on such a project at its atomic research center.

To focus the attention of our people on the benficient potentialities of atomic energy, the University of Michigan has proposed that the first Monday in October be observed throughout the nation as ATOM DAY.

Therefore, I, G. Mennen Williams, Governor of the State of Michigan, do hereby proclaim Monday, October 2, 1950, as ATOM DAY in Michigan, and urge all our people on that day and every day thereafter to aid in putting atomic energy to work as an instrument for the good of all the peoples of the world.

Given under my hand and the Great Seal of the State of Michigan, this twenty-seventh day of September, in the Year of Our Lord, One Thousand Nine Hundred Fifty, and the Commonwealth of the One Hundred Fourteenth.

G. Mennen Williams
Governor

Urges State To Support Phoenix Plan

Monday To Mark Campaign Start

Stressing that the world must learn to live with the atom before it can benefit from the new power Gov. G. Mennen Williams yesterday proclaimed Monday "Atom Day" throughout the state.

The Governor's proclamation gives official recognition to the start of the nation-wide fund raising campaign for the Michigan Memorial Phoenix Project Monday.

GOV. WILLIAMS turned the proclamation over to Marv Lubeck '51, chairman of the student Phoenix drive, and Betty Bridges, '52 chairman of the sororities' drive on campus, who had made the trip to Lansing for the ceremony.

In his statement, Gov. Williams urged the people of Michigan to use Atom day as a starting date for a continual effort to make atomic energy work for the good of mankind.

"If these forces (of atomic energy) are to build rather than destroy, they must be identified and controlled. The sooner we learn to live with the atom, the sooner will we benefit by the now incredible potentialities of atomic science," the message said.

IN THE MEANTIME Phoenix officials here were working out details of plans with the State Department which would send the special Atom Day program around the world on the Voice of America.

The program, which will feature talks by Gordon Dean, chairman of the Atomic Energy Commission, General Dwight Eisenhower, president of Columbia University and Warren Austin, United States ambassador to the United Nations, will be carried by Voice of America stations on Oct. 9 and 10.

Monday, the story of the opening of the drive for $6,500,000, which will turn plans for the memorial atomic research center into reality, will be told on regular newscasts sent by the "Voice."

Final details for the day's program are still being added by project directors.

ATOM DAY PROCLAIMED—Gov. G. Mennen Williams signs his Atom Day proclamation as Marv Lubeck and Betty Bridges, members of the Phoenix Project student executive committee, and H. E. Crouse, state chairman for the drive, look on. The Governor proclaimed Monday as Atom Day, and urged citizens to aid in putting atomic energy to work for peace.

Communists In Full Rout, Army Says

Taejon Liberated By Troops of UN

BULLETIN

TOKYO—(AP)—General MacArthur today turned over to South Korean President Syngman Rhee the capital city of Seoul.

TOKYO—(AP)—General Douglas MacArthur was reported parading in the streets of Seoul today in a victory celebration with South Korean President Syngman Rhee while elsewhere army officials reported the North Korean Army in complete rout and no longer an organized force.

Preparations for the victory parade have been under way for several days and a 50-piece marine band was assembled for the occasion.

AP CORRESPONDENT O. H. P. King reported from Seoul that the marine musicians served as litter bearers for the wounded while waiting to play the victory march.

The general is expected to hold conferences there on the probability of United Nations forces crossing the 38th parallel, which divided North and South Korea when the war broke on June 25.

The forces he commands were only a few miles from the parallel.

BRIG. GEN. Kong Nam Bong, operations officer for the Republic's forces, predicted his troops would reach the 38th parallel within 24 hours. An Eighth Army communique said two divisions of South Korean troops were within 45 miles of the parallel.

Meanwhile United Nations forces conducting a huge mop-up operation in the south recaptured Taejon, highway and rail hub 90 miles south of Seoul; Namwon, 42 miles northwest of Chinju and Hadong, 20 miles southeast of Chinju.

With the recapture of Taejon came a flickering of hope that Maj. Gen. William F. Dean, missing commander of the U.S. 24th Division, might be alive as a Red prisoner.

Dean was last reported outside Taejon July 21, just after his cut-up division had abandoned the town.

The U.S. Eighth Army commander, Lt. Gen. Walton H. Walker, told war correspondents at his South Korean headquarters:

"The North Korean army is in complete rout and no longer exists as an organized force."

THE AIR FORCE, however, reported that the North Koreans are continuing to build air fields north of the 38th parallel despite the disintegration of their army in South Korea.

Walker estimated that of the once overwhelming Red force of 150,00 men in South Korea, more than three-fourths have been or will be destroyed.

Those who escaped the trap were fleeing headlong to the north.

THE NEW Delhi radio broadcast a report that North Korean Premier Kim Il Sung has ordered all such Red troops as are able to return north of the 38th parallel.

'Ensian Picture Deadline Nears

Appointments for senior and graduate pictures should be made as soon as possible at the 'Ensian business office on the second floor of the Student Publications Bldg., said Clarence Kettler, business manager.

Photographers will be here on Monday, Oct. 2, and will remain only as long as there is continuous work to be done, he said.

The report reported that no pictures could be taken after Oct. 5, was erroneous, Kettler added.

No Rally Tonight

Hastily drawn plans for a pre-State pep rally dissolved yesterday as University officials advised SL and the Wolverine Club, co-sponsors of the measure, to substitute a better planned, better publicized rally before some future game.

Kagawa Urges Change Of Man To Beat A-Bomb

The only hope the world has of surviving the atomic bomb is the remaking of man, Tokohiko Kagawa, famed Japanese reformer, declared to a Hill Auditorium audience last night.

"And the only way mankind can be remolded is by an awakening consciousness of God," Kagawa said.

THE JAPANESE EVANGELIST warned that man can not dream of changing his present status unless he changes his heart.

Kagawa, who has served as a political and economic advisor to his government, warned that unless advanced man lends his hand to the backward of the earth there is no chance that democracy can ever exist.

"The best method of eliminating class differences betwen progressives and conservatives is for progressive classes to attempt to pull their opponents up to their level even if it means stooping down," he said.

However, he stressed that material betterment alone was not the answer to destroying the threat of atomic warfare.

KAGAWA URGED a union of science with religious thought and a reawakening of Christianity, which he termed the only means of reforming man.

"But today too many people lift the cross to the alter without knowing the meaning of it."

Recalling his message to the new government of Japan, he explained that Christianity was not just a dead doctrine.

"AS I TOLD our leaders when they accepted the Christian spirit as our standard of ethics, you must have the living spirit of God or your standards are no better than before."

He hailed the spirit of Christ through the ages as the great floor that has held Christianity together in spite of many mistakes on the part of the Christians.

"Christ suffered with God the sins of man; until we lose some sleep in the same suffering, our future is dim," he said.

Students Get AEC Positions

Four University students have been appointed predoctoral fellows for studies leading to eventual Atomic Energy Commission assignments, AEC announced yesterday.

The four are Paul R. Barker, Grad.; Frank E. Driggers, Grad.; Morton Fuchs, Grad; and George F. Bradley. All are studying physical science here.

Altogether, 11 men in the state received the AEC appointments.

In addition to the four now studying at the University, two others will study here under the AEC assignments. They are John V. Slater, of Willow Village, who will study biological science here, and Joshua Chover, of Detroit, who will study physical science.

'Not Guilty,' Alumnus Says

DETROIT—(AP)—William F. Welke, 24-year-old University graduate, pleaded innocent yesterday to a charge of extorting $3,500 from the wife of a Detroit physician.

Police said Welke has admitted obtaining money from Mrs. Katherine Vasu on May 31, 1949, by a telephone call threatening the life of her son, Cordell. Young Vasu resided in the same dormitory with Welke on the University campus.

Negro Issue May Split Fraternity

The University of Connecticut chapter of Phi Epsilon Pi fraternity has threatened to leave the national organization if it is refused authority to admit a Negro, according to the United Press.

The student, Alfred R. Rogers, was recently "blackballed" by the fraternity's national grand council.

World News Roundup

By The Associated Press

WASHINGTON — President Truman yesterday named Robert A. Lovett, diplomat, airman and Wall Street banker, as Deputy Secretary of Defense.

He succeeds Stephen T. Early who is leaving the No. 2 defense post Saturday to return to private business.

BERLIN—German police under British orders clubbed defiant Communists out of their luxurious headquarters in Duesseldorf yesterday. In a twin move also aimed at Ruhr Communists, the British summoned military reinforcements to deal with the threat of Ruhr-wide Red riots on Sunday.

NEW YORK — UN Security Council late yesterday turned down another Russian demand that Red China be invited to take part in U.N. discussions.

The vote on the specific question of inviting the Chinese Communists here to present their complaints that the United States had invaded China territory by sending the Seventh U.S. Fleet to patrol the Strait of Formosa.

WASHINGTON — President Truman yesterday picked George J. Bott to be General Counsel of the National Labor Relations Board.

Bott, who has been Associate General Counsel since 1948, was named to succeed Robert N. Denham, who resigned at White House request. Denham had been at odds with members of the

Army To Draft 300,000 Men In Six Months

WASHINGTON—(AP)—The Army yesterday announced plans to draft 300,000 men in the next six months.

This is in addition to 50,000 summoned in September which was the first month of the draft program touched off by the Korean outbreak and the vast defense undertaking.

PREVIOUSLY, the Army had called on selective service to supply 120,000 men in October and November.

Thus the 300,000 to be inducted in the next six months represents an increase of 180,000 over the pending draft calls already announced.

It raises the Army's total draft program to 350,000.

ON CAPITOL HILL, Chairman Vinson (D-Ga) of the House Armed Services Committee reported that the Army in the next six months will draft 1,400 dentists and 2,500 doctors, and call up 700 doctors in the reserve.

Washtenaw county's Draft Board announced that its November induction quota has been set at 70 men—12 more than the October call.

President Declares U.S. Must Not Cut Defenses

WASHINGTON—(AP)—President Truman said yesterday the United States must not let its guard down, now that the Korean fighting is nearing a victorious close.

He told his weekly news conference he is very happy about the success of the forces routing the North Korean Communists. He said he hopes it will wind up with a peace satisfactory to everybody.

BUT he agrred with General Omar N. Bradley, Chairman of the Joint Chiefs of Staff, that the greatest danger facing the United States is that it may let its guard down after the war is over.

The President predicted there would be what he called sincere efforts in Congress to block defense programs now under way, when the fighting ceases.

But he said it would not be Administration forces doing the blocking and he hopes the effort will not succeed, although the program will take money.

TRUMAN parried questions whether American forces would pursue fleeing north Koreans across the 38th parallel dividing North and South Korea. He couldn't answer that now because that line had not been reached, he said.

Other officials have said the resolution gives MacArthur authority to cross the parallel if necessary to destroy the Communist army.

Name Senior Daily Editors

Three appointments to senior staff positions on The Daily were announced last night by the Board in Control of Student Publications.

Nancy Bylan, '51, a history major from Grand Rapids, was appointed associate editor. Miss Bylan will take charge of training new sophomore Daily staff members.

SEE PICTURE PAGE 2

Also appointed to an associate editor post was James Gregory, '51. Gregory, an English major from Battle Creek, is a member of Theta Delta Chi fraternity. His new job involves training members of The Daily old sophomore staff.

Paul Schaible, '51BAd, was named to the post of advertising manager of The Daily. Schaible, a member of Delta Sigma Pi fraternity, is from Chelsea, Michigan.

INSPECTS ROTC UNIT:

Air Forces General Visits 'U' Campus

The University underwent a first-class military inspection yesterday when Major General Harry Johnson, Commanding Officer of the Tenth Air Force, visited the campus.

Accompanied by his military aides, Gen. Johnson inspected ROTC facilities on the campus, recorded a broadcast for WUOM, and visited President Ruthven for a short time.

Explaining that the main purpose of his visit was "only to orientate myself with ROTC facilities at Michigan," Gen. Johnson described the campus as "rather large" and the university's reserve officer training program as "adequate."

The commanding officer's visit was only one of 31 other trips he will make to universities in 13 states that include the ROTC program in their curricula. All these schools are included in the Tenth Air Force extending from Indiana to Colorado.

While he reported a need in the reserve corp for technically trained men with backgrounds in engineering, physics, or business administration, Gen. Johnson said there are no plans at present to extend ROTC facilities on the uni-

—Daily—Carlisle Marshall

MILITARY VISIT—Major Gen. Harry Johnson, Commanding Officer of the Tenth Air Force, exchanges greetings with President Ruthven while visiting the campus yesterday. General Johnson inspected ROTC facilities here and made a short broadcast over ... the ROTC program.

CENTENNIAL CONFERENCE:

Modernization Called Aim of Med School

"The future aims of the University Medical School are to modernize medical education to meet the changing needs of the present world," Dean Albert C. Furstenberg decl[illegible] night.

Dean Fur[illegible] address, "Aims and O[illegible] the Medical Faculty," c[illegible] first day of the Medical School's Centennial Union. He spoke at the Union before a gathering of more than ... people.

"... tion, will be the first step in achieving this modernization of medical education," Dean Furstenberg said.

"The clinic will place the medical student in a position where his academic education may be closely integrated with the practical side of his studies," the Medical School dean pointed out.

Dean Furstenberg also revealed that construction was soon to begin on the New Medical Research building will have facilities for 105 laboratories and house a 150,000 volume library," the Dean said.

OTHER speakers on the program were President Alexander G. Ruthven, who gave a toast of greeting to the alumni; Dr. Frederick G. Novy, who discussed the early developments of the Medical School; and Dr. Udo J. Wile, who outlined the recent history of the Medical School. Dr. Wile illustrated his talk with slides of

26

1950

In 1950, *The Michigan Daily* continued to expand their vertical column-based grid with the addition of an eighth column. However, unlike the previous grid systems, the *Daily* increased both their incorporation of photography and structural diversity of the story layout. Looking back to 1930, the *Daily* returns to a single bolded headline that consumes the width of the page. What is different from 1930 is the additional column, and the way in which headlines, photographs, and stories experiment with column width throughout the page. Examples of this are dispersed throughout the page. on the bottom left is a headline that spans three columns, on the bottom right there is a three column story, there is a three column photo on the upper right, and a two column blurb in the upper left.

1960

The 1960's mark a transitional period for *The Michigan Daily*. The grid is being partially broken, and the stories are chopped and fit together like a game of Tetris--cropped into odd shapes to accomodate the density of an eight column grid of text. On the bottom right, notice the story titled "Sterensom Blasts..." and note the way in which the beginning of the story is awkwardly interupted by the large, five column square story in the bottom center. A record number of three photographs appear, yet the thin single column nature of the top two are not condusive to photography. The top stories struggle to find a hierarchy* because of the displacement of the leading headline, which is pushed to the right five columns.

---

* The arrangement or presentation of elements in a way that implies importance.

The Michigan Daily

Seventy Years of Editorial Freedom

DOES PROGRAM NEED EXPANSION? See Page 4

PARTLY CLOUDY High—70 Low—45 Chance of showers in late afternoon of evening

VOL. LXXI, No. 9 — ANN ARBOR, MICHIGAN, THURSDAY, SEPTEMBER 29, 1960 — FIVE CENTS — EIGHT PAGES

Civil Rights Group Involved in Dispute

Louisiana Officials Deny Charges Of Unfair Treatment to Negroes

NEW ORLEANS (&P)—The United States Civil Rights Commission ended its hearings of Negro voter discrimination charges here yesterday in a stormy exchange with Louisiana Attorney General Jack Gremillion.

At the same time, Louisiana vote registrars and other officials, who over charges leveled against them, fired an angry barrage of telegrams at the six-member fact-finding body.

Gremillion, who attended the two-day hearings as an observer, asked to read a statement.

"We're not going to let you make a speech, Mr. Gremillion," Commission Vice-Chairman Robert A. Storey said. Storey said commission rules required statements be submitted 24 hours in advance.

"Are you going to let me read this statement?" Gremillion asked a second time.

Faces Trial

"We don't think it's legal," Storey said. "If you want to be a witness, and let us examine you that will be all right. But you cannot make a speech."

"Thank you for ruling me out of order," Gremillion said and sat down.

The volatile attorney general, who last month called a three-judge federal tribunal a "kangaroo court," faces a criminal contempt of court trial next week.

He later told newsmen he did not appear as a witness because the discrimination charges were not against him but against other state and parish (county) officials.

Hear Complaints

The commission heard 35 Negroes testify unequal application of the voter qualification law, disqualification on a host of minor points, and, in some cases, the threat of violence has held Louisiana's Negro registration down to 28 per cent of those eligible.

Eighty-two per cent of eligible white voters are registered.

The commission said it had received upwards of 150 voter complaints from Negroes in 17 of the state's 64 parishes. Most complaints came from rural northern parishes.

In his unread statement, Gremillion said officials had another version of the voting picture and suggested the commission should hear the other side of the story as well.

Defends Position

"You have provided opportunity to hear complaints ... I solicit equal opportunity and hearing under the same conditions the voters registrars and other public officials," Gremillion said in the statement.

Former state police chief Jack Nix Brown, in a telegram to the commission, said testimony he threatened the life of a Negro who tried to vote was a "false statement." Brown sent a copy of the wire to the state attorney general.

Denies Negro Story

Dist. Atty. John A. Richardson of Schreveport said no one in the Caddo parish district attorney's office had ever denied a Negro the right to vote. And "no Negro has complained to this office," Richardson added.

A telegram from Gremillion gave newsmen refuted testimony by Dr. John I. Reddix, Negro dentist from Monroe, who testified he had been purged and never been able to vote.

Chief Says U.S. Ready For Attack

NEW YORK (&P) — Air Force Gen. Nathan F. Twining said yesterday this country "can now defeat Russia, and China, if we are attacked, and the Communist leaders know it."

He later told newsmen he is retiring Oct. 1 as chairman of the Joint Chiefs of Staff, added in an address prepared for a dinner of the National Security Industrial Association.

"They know that even if they launched a surprise attack, they would bring down certain destruction on their own heads.

"A nuclear world is not a desirable world, but it is preferable, to my thinking, to a communized lid. The American capability for waging war-winning response over attacks must be kept sure, whatever the costs. It is the only real guarantee of the peace, one that cannot win will not come.

"Training forecast a cold war blood that could last for years.

"It will go on until there is a clear winner and a clear loser. The struggle is too big, too vast, too deadly for compromise," he said the nation's top military man said.

"All of you, as responsible citizens, might make more noise, and the press and your government will, even if you understand that certain tensions are the cause of elements—not the reverse—and any meaningful disarmament only follow—not precede—political reconciliation."

Paper To Sue CNY Head Over Slander

NEW YORK (&P)—The President of City College disclosed yesterday that a student newspaper he has accused of following a "marxist line" is considering a slander suit against him.

Buell G. Gallagher, who is the original charge against the newspaper Observation Post in a news conference last week, said another news conference yesterday:

"I read to newsmen the part of open letter which will appear in the student newspaper, calling for immediate and open action of the general faculty to disavow the newspaper called Gallagher's 'slanderous accusations.'

"The student editorial also said newspaper would seek censure against Gallagher, and that said editor said he had been ordered by the editorial board to investigate possible legal action."

Peace Talks Open in Laos

VIENTIANE (&P) — Peace talks started at settling Laos' 18-day-old civil war opened yesterday in Luang Prabang.

"The military commanders of Prince Souvanna Phouma's rebel government and those of Gen. Phoumi Nosavan's right wing regime met in the royal capital to try to settle the political phase was expected to open today, if the commanders reach agreement.

"Western embassy official who said he was still in the dark as to what the talks were bringing said at the Royal Palace. Prince Souvanna said later any decision reached at Luang Prabang are subject to approval by the princes."

He had also instructions to delegation, made up of four or three colonels, were

---

PETITIONS:

Say Reds Promote U.S. Ruin

"The perpetrators of the most heinous conspiracy in the history of the world will verbally promote America's destruction among our nation's students," petitioners charged yesterday in their attempt to re-establish a speaking ban against Communists at Wayne State University.

"The Communists are our natural enemies and we should treat them that way," Anne Byerlein, one of the two organizers of the protest campaign said. She and Donald Lobsinger are hoping to present 25,000 petition signatures to WSU President Clarence B. Hilberry by October 11. Neither one is affiliated with Wayne, or has attended classes there.

8,000 petitions each containing space for 25 signatures have been

[photo caption:]
CLARENCE B. HILBERRY
... welcomes speakers

mailed but throughout the state in response to requests for them, Miss Byerlein said. There are still a lot of patriotic citizens in Michigan," she added, noting that several petitions had been sent to Ann Arbor.

The petitions began circulating Saturday at a Republican party rally in Detroit, where N.Y. Governor Nelson Rockefeller signed one under a sign reading "Stop Communist Subversion at Wayne State University." Cries of "Don't let America be destroyed at Wayne State University" and "Don't let Khrushchev come to Wayne" urged people to sign the protest letter.

The 10 year policy of excluding Communist speakers from WSU's campus was revoked 13 days ago by Wayne's Board of Governors. Hilberry told the Board, "The university has an obligation to analyze in a scientific manner the major issues of the day. This is the way it fulfills its responsibility to develop the leaders of tomorrow.

"Accordingly the university welcomes outside speakers whose competencies are relevant to its research and instructional programs ... the responsibility for sound judgment as to whether their contributions will be consistent with the functions of the University rests, with the individual faculty member, the dean of the college, the dean of students, or the president depending on the specific occasion."

New Yorkers Give Nixon Big Ovation

Pulls Small Crowds In Greater New York

NEW YORK (&P)—Vice President Richard M. Nixon received the longest, loudest, wildest ovation of his campaign for President last night to cap his first invasion of key New York State.

And this was at the end of a day that began with the smallest, coolest turnout the Republican nominee for the White House had encountered so far.

From morning until past dusk, Nixon zig-zagged over miles of political paths in greater New York — in Manhattan and on neighboring Long Island.

Only Few

In the borough of Queens, just across the East River from the great city's skyscrapers, Nixon pulled only a few hundred persons in rallies along his motorcade route. But then several thousands turned out at the Nassau County courthouse in Mineola, more thousands at a shopping center at Hicksville, and then tonight—a wall-bulging throng at the Long Island Arena. And at Commack, perhaps the largest indoor crowd of the campaign gave the Vice President a reception the likes of which he could not recall.

Grinning from ear to ear, Nixon commented "it's like the Republican national convention and you've even outdone them."

It was the first time a presidential candidate of either party had appeared in Suffolk County.

'Not Last'

"I can tell you," Nixon exclaimed, "on the basis of what I've seen, it sure won't be the last."

A couple of police officers took a look at the crowd and estimated 9,000 or 10,000 persons were crammed into the arena, with 3,000 to 6,000 hanging around outside, and unable to squeeze in. There was a large proportion of teenagers, some with placards saying "if we could vote, we'd vote Nixon."

Loudest Crowd

There wasn't much question that it was the loudest crowd Nixon had encountered. The minute he and his wife Pat walked onto the stage the partisans were on their feet shrieking, yelling, beating drums, chanting and waving hundreds of splashy-colored paper pompons on the ends of sticks.

For 6½ minutes the demonstration thundered on. And then when the Vice President was formally introduced, there were two more minutes of bedlam.

Nixon Stumps New York City As Kennedy Campaigns Upstate

RAWICKE SPEAKS:

Presidential Candidates Sidestepped Vital Issues

By MICHAEL BURNS

Taking a blast at Kennedy and Nixon for avoiding the issues in their televised debate, Prof. George Rawicke of the Wayne State University history department, began his discussion of "The National Elections: Do We Have a Real Choice?"

"Nothing seemed to be said" by either candidate with regard to the real issues, the speaker told the Democratic Socialists last night.

In discussing the question of peace, they talked instead about military expenditures and defensive measures. They did not discuss in an intelligent matter the Cuban or African situations, the Socialist said. The politicians tend to place all countries into two categories: those for us and those against us—and the neutralists are thought of as enemies.

PROF. GEORGE RAWICKE
...candidate evasion

Nixon and Kennedy skirted the issues on minimum wage and public housing questions, Prof. Rawicke said. They debated the wage policy of those organizations making over $1 million a year, neglecting the millions of employees who are most affected working in small service concerns and being underpaid.

Public housing policy has taken a trend toward building middle-class dwellings, rather than the vitally-needed low-income projects. He charged that present construction programs are breeding more ghettoes than eliminating them.

This uncommitted and inactive approach to politics by the major parties has bred an indifference and even rejection in politics by the students. They wish to dis-associate with the bureaucracy and "swindle" of government.

'U' Sets Plan To Process Complaints

The University has adopted a written procedure for handling the non-academic employes at the University Hospital.

A similar plan will go into effect within the dental department as soon as procedural details are worked out. Wilbur K. Pierpont, vice-president in charge of business and finance said yesterday.

The written grievance procedure, a "formalizing and detailing of existing informal and unwritten procedures, was the result of discussion by University personnel officials with representatives of the Building Service Employee International Union, Local 378, and with those of the American Federation of State, County and Municipal Employees Unions, Local 1583.

The University has also made arrangements for payroll deduction of union dues for members of both unions. Deductions will be made only on the written request of an employee.

The first dues deduction will be made from October pay checks.

The Regents approved the institution of a dues check-off system after State Attorney General Paul Adams ruled that it was legally possible for a state agency such as the University to do so.

Membership in either union is entirely voluntary.

Status of Students as Voters in Ann Arbor Defined by Attorney at SGC's Request

At the request of the Student Government Council last spring, City Attorney Jacob F. Fahrner, Jr., prepared a statement of the status of students as voters in Ann Arbor.

His opinion regarding students' eligibility was presented last night to SGC at their regular meeting.

The Michigan Election Laws state that no elector shall be deemed to have gained or lost a residence while a student at any institution of learning.

Whether or not the student may regard the University as his home is also stated: "The great weight of authority is that 'a student at college who is free from parental control, regards the place where the college is situated as his home, has no other to which to return in case of sickness ... is as much entitled to vote as any other residents. ..."

Some of the factors which City Clerk Fred J. Looker considers in determining eligibility are as follows:

1) Whether the student is married and has established his own home with his wife in Ann Arbor and remains in that home during the time that school is not in session.

2) The length of stay in Ann Arbor. 3) Whether the student is free from parental control. 4) Where he would go in case of sickness or accident. 5) If employed, the amount of time devoted to gainful employment in relation to academic pursuits.

Nancy Adams, executive vice-president of SGC, who spearheaded the clarification of voting rights, said that she felt that "this is a sign of real cooperation between the city and the University." She said she felt that the matter could now be cleared up without further conflict.

Thousands See Senator In Rochester

Democrat Says GOP 'Blocks Progress'

WASHINGTON (&P)— Both Sen. John F. Kennedy and Vice President Richard M. Nixon parked them in yesterday as they battled for New York's 45 presidential electoral votes—the nation's biggest bloc.

The two presidential candidates didn't cross paths Nixon, the GOP nominee, swung through metropolitan New York while Kennedy, the Democratic candidate, invaded upstate New York.

Wild Ovation

In suburban Suffolk County, Nixon received a wild ovation in an indoor speech at Commack. Nixon said it surpassed the reception he got from the 1960 Republican National convention at Chicago.

Dense, uproarious crowds greeted Kennedy in upstate Rochester, an appearance as large as in Ohio Tuesday when Gov. Michael LaSalle estimated that close to 700,000 cheered him on a 200-mile tour.

Kennedy brought a roar of laughter from a capacity crowd of 10,000 at Rochester War Memorial Auditorium when he quipped, "I didn't know Rochester was such a strong Democratic city."

Rochester usually is considered a Republican stronghold President Dwight D. Eisenhower won solid majorities there in 1952 and 1956.

Buffalo Address

Continuing his drive to win New York's crucial 45 electoral votes for the presidency, Kennedy came out slapping at his GOP rival in an address to a dinner of "senior citizens" in Buffalo.

Nixon not only led the opposition, Kennedy declared, but he was "ready to carry on that opposition when picked by the Republican national convention to head its ticket.

"In 1935, the Republican failed to block progress," the Democratic presidential nominee said in his prepared speech.

'Destroy Hopes'

"This year they succeeded in destroying the hopes of Americans over the age of 65 for relief from the crushing burden of medical bills and for the opportunity to fully care for their health."

Instead of a program for medical care under the social security system, Kennedy said, the Republicans substituted a bill "which will cost the American taxpayer over a billion dollars a year, is impossible to administer, which will not even be put into effect in many of our states, which has been rejected by the Governor of New York, and which fails to bring relief where it does go into effect."

"Only with a Democratic president in the White House, can we hope to bring help to poverty-stricken older Americans.

"And in 1961," he told the audience of "Democratic President, And in 1961, help will be on the way," Kennedy noted that, in the televised "great debate" of Monday night, Nixon described Democratic plans for medical care as "extreme."

Kennedy added that he did not believe it was "extreme" to relieve poverty and illness through the tested social security system.

"When the Republican Party nominated Mr. Nixon, they not only elected a leader—they selected a man whose record has proved him to be a true leader and representative of this historic Republican tradition—a man who led the opposition to medical care for the aged, and a man who was ready to carry on that opposition."

Stevenson Blasts GOP For 'Losing Initiative'

LOS ANGELES (&P)—Adlai Stevenson last night described Vice President Richard Nixon as "not a leader, but a misleader" who "takes every catastrophe in his stride."

Stevenson returned to the city where he won the biggest ovation of the 1960 Democratic convention—but not the nomination—to stump on behalf of the man who won the bid.

In a speech prepared for delivery tonight at Shrine Auditorium, the two-time Democratic candidate for President accused the Republican administration of having "lost the initiative for peace" and not conquering problems "before they become crises."

He broached a serious question on disarmament: Whether it should be a matter of "top priority" in United States foreign affairs.

He had kind words for Democratic candidate Sen. John Kennedy—and many less-than-kind for his Republican opponent:

Nixon, he declared, "calls the record of Republican failure 'experience' and solemnly advances it as a reason for the people choosing him as President."

Discusses Experience

"Experience can be a form of recommendation, all right. But the experience growing out of a long series of calamities recommends only that the person involved be retired as soon as possible to a place where he can do no future harm—such as, for example, private life."

Stevenson asked if the United States "should stand still, or should it press forward again? Or by failing to apply new remedies, will we produce new evils?

Provides Answer

"To this question the Republican candidate has provided his answer. He has gone around the country singing a single lullaby. His song has been everything is fine, there is nothing to worry about—but don't change administrations in these dangerous times!

"The Republican campaign is, in essence, to arouse the fear and contentment—to anesthetize the people in the face of foaming revolutions of our time."

IQC PRESIDENT GIVES ENDORSEMENT:

Undergraduate Men Prepare for Annual Fall Rush

By MICHAEL OLINICK

"When I was a rushee, I used to see just how many bids we could get before we accepted one," Inter-Fraternity President Jon Trost, '61, said last night.

Welcoming more than 700 undergraduate men who attended a large but smokeless Mass Open Rush Meeting at the Union, Trost warned them to "make sure the house you pledge is the one you want to pledge."

"A hearty" endorsement of men's rush was given by the representative of the University's 3,500 quadrangle residents, Dan Rosemergy, '61. The Inter-Quadrangle Council president said he believed "Every man should have this experience. There is enough space at Michigan for every kind of living accommodation. We have one of the finest fraternity systems in the country and one of the best residence hall organizations." Many of the fraternity men present could not recall a previous time when a Quadrangle official publicly advocated rush.

Rosemergy, however, asked the rushees to be fair and careful. "Don't jump in with your eyes closed," he warned.

Coordination Effort

Robert Peterson, '62, IFC Rushing Chairman, claimed Peterson "has done more than any other person to coordinate the residence halls and the Michigan fraternities."

"Beware of the early bid and the hot box," Trost warned. "Rush is a fascinating and unique experience and it's a two-week period. Let's remember that.

"When an offer to become a pledge of a certain fraternity is made, it is not retractable, and you need not accept it on the spot. Speaking for the 44 Michigan fraternity presidents, may I recommend you wait until the second Monday of rush before you accept a bid."

Theta Delta Sing

Speaking after the identically dressed Theta Delta Chi choir sang its award-winning rendition of "Sea Chanty Medley," Trost claimed one of the goals of the fraternity was "personal development of the individual, mind and body. We are concerned with the moral ... We stress the qualities are human

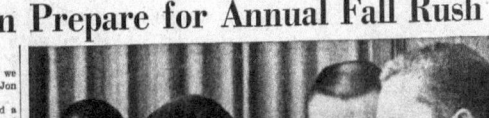

EXPLAIN RUSH—Robert Peterson, Interfraternity Council rush chairman; Louis Rice, assistant dean of men; Dan Rosemergy, Inter-Quadrangle president; and Jon Trost, IFC president, talked to

---

Campus Party Calls Meeting

A mass meeting of the prospective campus political party will take place at 7:30 p.m. today in the Henderson room of the League.

Within the week, the party's organizing committee will announce a written platform on which to run candidates in the forthcoming all-campus Student Government Council election. Daily Editor Thomas Hayden, '61, will discuss the need for a party on campus and the issues with which it might become involved.

LOMBARDI: A HOLLOW LEGACY
See Page 7

The Michigan Daily

IMPROVING
Partly cloudy, warmer
High—67
Low—40

[illegible] No. 24 | Ann Arbor, Michigan — Wednesday, September 30, 1970 | Ten Cents | Eight Pages

Academic reform: Students take the initiative

By ROB SCHREINER and EDWARD ZIMMERMAN

[illegible] Winter, 1969, the dispute [illegible] literary college's language [illegible] requirement was able to bring a [illegible] number of students to [illegible] an issue which has rare[illegible] a focus of campus politics [illegible] issue of academic reform.

[illegible] year-and-a-half later, the [illegible] for altering many aspects of [illegible] life at the University [illegible] been submerged under a flurry [illegible] popular social issues such [illegible] minority admissions and the [illegible] University's ties with the military. [illegible] as campus-wide political [illegible] prepare for another year [illegible] the blunted quest for [illegible] change has been rele[illegible] to smaller, less conspicuous [illegible] groups within almost [illegible] school, college and department.

Although the aims of the groups are diverse, they have traditionally centered around two general areas: Changing the decision-making mechanism within their academic unit to include greater student participation; and pressing for specific decisions on academic issues.

In a series of recent interviews representatives of the groups have described the issues which will concern them this year as including:

—**Curricular reform.** This will continue to be of the greatest concern to the student groups; they say it is the area which affects them the most. As the term progresses, many departmental student groups have begun to press for vast changes in the concentration requirements. The major departments involved are history, English and economics.

—**Grading.** The extension of the pass-fail grading system is an item on the agenda of almost every student group. While some students are pushing to make all courses in their units pass-fail, the majority [illegible] such as the Student Council in the business administration school—seek to end letter grading in certain courses only.

—**Admissions.** With the establishment last spring of a University-wide minority admissions program, many of the student groups plan to press their academic unit to establish special programs which will aid the new black students to adjust to the University.

In addition, some groups such as the Graduate Association of Political Scientists, have begun to recruit minority students.

—**The Budget.** This is an area in each school and department which the faculty has usually preferred to handle alone. However, the financial overtones of the minority admissions dispute has prompted some student groups to seek participation in the setting of priorities for allocating their unit's funds.

—**Tenure.** This area—the hiring, promotion and dismissal of faculty members—is the one aspect of academics in which the students have virtually no participation in the University. Yet most student groups indicate they are hesitant to take up the issue, fearing that the faculty will be intransigent on other issues if students press for more influence in tenure decisions.

"There are more important concerns without arousing the faculty's ire over so emotional an issue," says Randy Beers, a member of the history students steering committee.

Related to these substantive academic issues is the question of student participation in the actual decision-making within each academic unit.

In most schools, colleges and departments decisions on the appointment and promotion of faculty members, and on budgetary matters are handled by an executive committee elected by the faculty. Other faculty committees have jurisdiction over other areas such as curriculum.

In past years, student efforts in academic reform have focused on gaining representation on these bodies. Many faculty committees have responded by seating some students in an advisory or a voting capacity.

This year, the majority of student groups seem to be satisfied with the extent of their representation, saying that even non-voting participation allows them a significant input into the system.

For this reason, student leaders say, most of their reform efforts this year will be aimed at the actual decisions made by the faculty bodies, rather than the decision-making process itself.

This term, the history department will resume debate on a proposal to change the program for graduate students. Under the proposal, the students would be required to take courses in only four historical fields, instead of five. They would also have wider latitude in deciding which courses to take.

Both graduate and undergraduate history students also plan to evaluate the department's placement program, which finds positions for graduate students after they receive their degrees.

In the political science department, the Undergraduate Political Science Association has been instrumental in the past in bringing about curricular changes, including the awarding of four credits for all courses and ending the requirement that a prospective major must take two political science courses as prerequisites for concentration.

Neil Gabler, president of the undergraduate association, says that this year the group will be concerned with the frequency of course offerings. It will attempt to assure that popular courses are

See ACADEMIC, Page 2

[illegible]AL TOMORROW:

[illegible]rabs mourn Nasser; [illegible]ideast status unclear

—Associated Press

[illegible]HELNI of the Egyptian army, left, meets in [illegible] officers of the Arab peacekeeping force named [illegible] cease-fire in Jordan. The meeting took place in [illegible]tinental Hotel.

CAIRO (P) — As the Arab world mourned the death of Gamal Abdel Nasser yesterday, world leaders wondered what effect his death will have on peace efforts in the Middle East.

Many feared the Egyptian president's death may mean a new setback for the already stalled peace talks between Israel and its Arab neighbors.

President Nixon, however, said it was too early to know how Nasser's death may affect the troubled Mideast. He told newsmen accompanying him to the U.S. 6th Fleet in the Mediterranean:

"It will contribute a new situation, but whether it contributes to more tension remains to be seen. I think it is much too early to say because we do not know whom his successor will be or whether it might be some kind of collective leadership."

Some diplomats at the United Nations said Nasser's death might spell the end of the U.S. initiative that laid the groundwork for the talks with a 90-day cease-fire between Israel on one side and Egypt and Jordan on the other. Gunnar V. Jarring, the U.S. peace mediator, disagreed, saying it was too early to tell, a U.N. spokesman reported.

Acting President Anwar Sadat received condolences from world leaders, some of whom began arriving for the state funeral on Thursday.

There was little speculation among Egyptians in their hour of mourning as to a successor to Nasser, but they learned that some of his closest advisers had been at his bedside, among them Sadat.

He was a fellow officer in the 1952 coup against the monarchy and was chosen by Nasser to be his vice president. He is acting president until a new chief executive is chosen within 60 days.

Others included Gen. Mohammed Fawzi, commander in chief of the armed forces, and Air Marshal Aly Sabri, a former confidant of Nasser.

With Sadat as chairman, the executive committee of Egypt's only political party, the Arab Socialist Union, and the Cabinet met in emergency session. It was presumed they discussed the date

See ARABS, Page 8

[illegible] march, rally [illegible]led for Oct. 3

By HANNAH MORRISON

[illegible]nti-war rally in Ann Arbor promises to be [illegible]tion in the country at that time," says Jim [illegible] of the Detroit Coalition to End the War.

[illegible]sponsored demonstration will begin as a [illegible]otball stadium after Saturday's game to [illegible]

[illegible] national Peace Action Coalition (PAC) [illegible]ress the rally on the Vietnam war, the [illegible]nd PAC's relation to those issues. Michael [illegible]atic candidate for Congress will also be [illegible]

[illegible]other anti-war demonstration is planned [illegible], to protest a "Victory in Vietnam" march [illegible]at date.

[illegible]al PAC has withdrawn support of the [illegible]ecause, Student Mobilization Committee [illegible] explains, [illegible] confron-[illegible]

[illegible] from col-[illegible] [illegible]'e met in [illegible] to discuss [illegible]ation and [illegible]n on Ann [illegible]

[illegible] in a col-[illegible] [illegible]e to kick [illegible]ies," Laf-[illegible]

[illegible] purpose [illegible]nd people [illegible]e is not [illegible]

[illegible] has held [illegible] to publi-[illegible] [illegible]he group [illegible] schools, [illegible]e down-[illegible]

[illegible] efforts [illegible] 31"—the [illegible] anti-war [illegible]s includ-[illegible]

[illegible] local [illegible]ent, he [illegible]

[illegible]it dem-[illegible] Satur-[illegible]

—Associated Press

MOURNERS CROWD the streets of Cairo yesterday, wishing to pay final tribute to Egyptian President Gamal Abdel Nasser. From all over Egypt crowds tried to reach Koubbeh, the Cairo suburb [illegible]

—Associated Press

Kent State memorial

Student Tim Butz, left, burns what was said to be a draft card at the close of a Monday night service at Kent State University. The service was in memory of the four students killed at the school May 4 in a confrontation with Ohio National Guardsmen. The Rev. Ralph Abernathy, president of the Southern Christian Leadership Conference, is at the right.

NEW 'U' LEGAL SYSTEM:

Judiciary unit deadlocked on makeup of procedural panel

By DAVE CHUDWIN

The committee formulating a new University judicial system was deadlocked last night on one of the few remaining issues as it attempted to finalize recommendations for a permanent legal system to replace present interim procedures.

Torpedoing hopes for approval of a general outline at the meeting, student, faculty and administration members of the committee disagreed on who should decide procedure in jury trials.

The committee, appointed by President Robben Fleming last April, previously approved the principle of trial by a jury of peers —students being tried and sentenced by students and an equivalent procedure for faculty members.

The problem blocking committee agreement is the composition of a panel to preside over hearings and to make procedural rulings on matters such as admissibility of evidence.

Student Government Council President Marty Scott emphasized the importance of such rulings, pointing out what Judge Julius Hoffman was able to do with questionable rulings in the Chicago conspiracy trial.

Some of the faculty members of the committee insisted their colleagues would have little faith in a system that has a student-dominated procedural panel as well as a jury.

The student representatives made clear their reluctance to approve any panel that is permanently faculty controlled and would decide procedural questions when students are defendants.

The committee's previous concensus — choosing the three-man panel by lot from an equal number of students and faculty — was apparently forgotten as six other plans were presented.

Among the alternatives are a panel of one student and one faculty member with an additional chairman elected by lot, a similar plan with the chairman an outside lawyer, a panel of two students with a faculty chairman and a panel of two faculty members with student chairman.

"Faculty members have prejudices that reflect their backgrounds," Law Prof. Theodore St. Antoine said. "In the terms of faculty acceptance, they would feel better with trained legal presence."

"What any system needs most is acceptability sufficient enough so that when procedural decisions adverse to one party are given, they will still be able to buy that system," Scott said later.

The committee has not yet been able to find a solution that is acceptable to both students and faculty factions of the group.

In a straw vote the entire committee agreed that each of the proposed systems for a procedural panel would be fair and impartial, would result in more competent rulings and which could be sold politically.

During the meeting Regent Robert Nederlander (D-Birmingham) suggested the committee might present the range of alternatives and reasoning behind them on the question to the Regents for them to decide.

Scott and Michael Davis, Grad, disagreed, saying the committee was charged with coming up with a recommendation. They added that to let the Regents choose alternatives would upset the delicate balance established — if a decision could be made.

After three hours of discussion the committee appeared no closer to agreement, and members to adjourn and consult their respective constituencies before next week's meeting.

Ask ruling on secrecy of Regents

By ROB BIER
Associate Managing Editor

In a move which could end the Regents' ability to meet in closed session, Rep. Jack Faxon (D-Detroit) yesterday sent a letter to state Atty. Gen. Frank Kelley requesting a ruling on the legality of the current regental practice.

The Regents typically spend approximately 14 hours in meetings at each monthly session, only four of which are open to the public. This is in apparent contradiction of a ruling made by Kelley in August, 1969 which states any meeting of the Regents for the transaction of business, held in accordance with the Regents own rules, must be open to the public.

The attorney general is legally obligated to make a ruling in response to a request from a state legislator, and that ruling has the force of law.

Faxon said the apparent contradiction first came to his attention two weeks ago through a Daily article citing specific actions taken by the Regents in closed session.

The Regents regularly act secretly on land transactions, appointments and honorary degrees and staff and faculty salaries. Although they usually take the actual vote at their brief public session, details of the matter being voted on are rarely disclosed and often a number of previously agreed-upon actions are approved as one.

Details of regental action are likewise kept out of the official minutes by referring only to numbered exhibits which are never described.

In his letter to Kelley, Faxon referred to the attorney general's earlier opinion and asked for a ruling on the following questions:

—Can the Board of Regents "exercise its constitutional or legal powers at a meeting from which the public is barred?"

—What is the legality of any transaction or business conducted at such a meeting?

—What is the responsibility of the Regents to keep complete minutes of all their actions and to make those minutes available to the public?

—Can the Regents legally conduct business by telephone, or by any other means which does not

See REP., Page 8

Fleming on youth panel

President Robben Fleming will participate in a White House Conference on Youth sometime late in February as co-chairman of a task force on education.

The group, also chaired by John Charles Thomas, a student from the University of Virginia, will present a report on education and youth to be discussed by conference participants.

"It's a conference in which there are eight or ten task forces on various issues such as drugs, education and poverty," Fleming explains. "Each task force has two co-chairmen, one over 25 years old and the other under."

Fleming and Thomas met with the other members of the group at the Irvine campus of the University of California for three days at the end of August to plan an outline of the education task force's report.

Fleming says he does not feel it inconsistent for him to attend a White House conference considering personal attacks on him by Vice President Spiro Agnew who alluded to Fleming as a "marshmallow."

"One who's interested in education doesn't make a decision on whether to attend a conference on the basis of what party is doing it," Fleming says.

NEW LAWS, NO FACILITIES

Abortion reform: Not enough

By The Associated Press

Abortion laws have now been liberalized in 15 states. But liberal doesn't always mean available.

It's still easier to get one if you are wealthy.

It's still easier to find out where to get one if you live in a large city and have a private doctor.

And it may take time. So much, that it would probably help to make the appointment before you get pregnant.

In short, women who previously jetted to Puerto Rico, or England, or Japan, can now taxi down to the corner hospital, where they probably will get their abortions. But for the women who couldn't afford the plane fare in the first place, the possibilities sink.

The nation's new mood of reform has not solved the abortion issue yet.

"You can have the most liberalized abortion law in the world, but it won't do any good without facilities and a hospital that allows it," says Mrs. Fred Schumacher, executive director of Planned Parenthood, in Washington, D.C.

Dr. Bernard Nathanson, an obstetrician [illegible] tion law reform, put it another way: "Sure, a woman under 24 weeks pregnant could get an abortion in New York today. But she'd probably be discouraged, disheartened, disillusioned, humiliated and broke."

With some modification, aspects of that statement describe all of the states which have broadened their abortion laws since 1967. True, abortions have increased spectacularly in some places: New York City's 15 municipal hospitals performed 1,281 during the first four weeks of that state's new law this summer as compared to about 581 for all of 1967. Maryland's 2,134 abortions during its first year of liberalization gave that state a ratio of 18 abortions per 1,000 live births—compared to the national ratio of 2 per 1,000.

But during those same periods, New York's municipal hospitals had to backlog 4,848 requests. Maryland turned down more than twice as many abortions as were performed. Colorado denied 19 of every 20 requests. And where abortions were performed, other problems were reported:

—High costs. Average fees run from $200 to [illegible]

30

1970

1970 marks a major divergence from *The Michigan Daily*'s previous design. They utterly abandon any set width or number of columns that was the crux of the previous newspaper designs. The top story is boxed off and has a horizontal format with seven short columns. On the bottom right of the page is a similarly boxed off section. However, this story only has two thick columns, taking up the space of three of the standard text columns above the box. The distance between the top columns is wider than the distance between the lower columns, meaning that they do not align. Notice that the lower far left column ends right in the center of the column above it. The photographs take up a much larger portion of the page, and serve as the new focal points.

1980

The Michigan Daily continues to separate the stories with boxes and rules in the 1980 cover, using a different column and grid format for each story. At the top of the page there are six columns, which then changes to five, then to four for the bottom two stories--completely isolating the text from story to story. There is also a wide range in text size and italicization for the headlines, creating separate and distinct spaces for each segment. This is the first example of the picture being displayed on the upper left-hand corner, a format that soon becomes standard practice. It is also the first example of the five story per page layout that exists to this day.

Ninety-One Years of Editorial Freedom

The Michigan Daily

Vol. ... No. 23 — Ann Arbor, Michigan, Tuesday, September 30, 1980 — Ten Cents — Twelve Pages

Daily Photo by JIM KRUZ

...YT serves an unidentified customer in the South Quad store which was the scene of a Sunday morning armed

Armed robbers hold up store in South Quad

By MAUREEN FLEMING

City police are looking for a pair of armed robbers who stole a few hundred dollars from the South Quad student store early Sunday morning.

Police Sgt. Harold Tinsey said the robbery, which occurred at 2 a.m. Sunday, is still under investigation.

Cashier Jim Davidson said a man made a purchase at the store and left. Another man entered the basement store, picked up a bag of Doritos and a black South Quad T-shirt.

THE FIRST MAN reentered the store, closing the door behind him. Davidson said the second man apparently wrapped a gun in the t-shirt before walking toward the register.

"He told me to give him the money in the register," Davidson continued. "At first I didn't understand him until he showed me the gun."

The robbers made Davidson lie on the floor and threatened to kill him. Davidson said they told him things like "We're dope addicts, we'll do anything for a fix."

"I NEVER REALLY thought I was going to get killed but I was afraid they would hit me on the head," he explained.

He said the robbery didn't seem very dangerous, adding "I'm not going to risk my life for a few hundred dollars."

Davidson said both robbers were between 20 and 22 years old. He said he was positive they were not South Quad residents and he didn't think they were University students.

DAVIDSON EXPLAINED that he isn't afraid to continue working at the store but he said he is "more wary of people I don't know coming in." He said he knows most of the people who come into the store.

Store manager Steve Gutterman said he proposed to make the store safer by cutting back the hours and making it less profitable for robbers.

He plans to cut back store hours from 2:00 a.m. to 1 a.m. Friday and Saturday. The new hours would be more consistent with the snack bar hours, Gutterman explained.

HE ADDED THAT he would like to see a "permanent drop safe" installed in the store. Once the cash register contains a certain amount of money, the cashier would put the money in a safe. The cashier would have no key, Gutterman said.

"Random patrols by security guards will be increased also," he added.

South Quad residents surveyed were either uninformed of the robbery or seemed unconcerned, although interested in the details.

ONE STORE employee who wished to remain unidentified said students who have come in and asked questions about the robbery were more interested than scared.

Laura Orlando, a West Quad freshwoman, confirmed the store employee's belief. "I can't say it makes me nervous . . . if it happens a couple more times I may get nervous," she said.

Orlando added that she wasn't surprised about the robbery "because there are all sorts of characters running around here."

A staff employee said the robbery surprised her since she hadn't heard anything about it. "The staff wasn't informed," she explained.

"I live here and I never heard about it," Maureen Drummond said. "It makes me nervous."

"So much has happened around here that you just ignore it and don't take any foolish risks," Diane Swonk added.

...aq will abide by U.N. ...ase-fire if Iran agrees

...from AP and UPI

...AD, Iraq—Iraq agreed ...to a U.N. call for a cease-... Iran did the same. But ...g did not subside. Iraqi ...equipment moved south-... toward the enemy's ...land, where Iranian ...appeared to have stif-...

...esident Saddam Hussein ...etter to U.N. Secretary-... Waldheim that Iraq ...e Security Council ap-... cease-fire if Iran also ...een urged the council to ...sary measures to urge ... side to abide" by the ...approved Sunday. Iran ...espond immediately to ...

...le, Egypt declared ...hat it supported U.N. in-... the Persian Gulf war ...s armed forces stood ...end the other Gulf coun-... attack.

...ides of President Anwar ...as called for American ... in the Iran-Iraq con-... reiterated an offer to give ...States "limited and temporary" military facilities in Egypt.

In other developments:

- IRAN'S ambassador to the Soviet Union, Mohammad Mokri, told a Moscow news conference Iran might agree to a cease-fire if Iraq's president resigned, Iraq's army surrendered, the Iraqi city of Basra were turned over to Iranian control pending an election there, and Iraq's Kurds were allowed to vote on whether they wanted autonomy or to join with Iran.
- Western diplomatic sources in London said yesterday that Japan, Britain, France, Italy, West Germany and France had agreed to a U.S. call for talks on keeping open Persian Gulf oil shipping lanes. The U.S. earlier said it would consider military force to ensure access to oil from the Gulf.
- A special envoy representing Iranian President Abolhassan Bani-Sadr met in New Delhi with Indian Prime Minister Indira Gandhi and said he urged her, as a leader in the non-aligned movement, to help end the war. The envoy, Shams Ardakani, said Cuba, the current chairman of the nonaligned bloc, also was playing a role, but he did not elaborate.
- A "goodwill" mission from the Islamic Conference arrived in Baghdad. The mission—headed by conference leaders President Mohammed Zia of Pakistan and conference Secretary—General Rabib el Chatti of Tunisia—was told by Iranian leaders earlier in Tehran that it would not be permitted to mediate the Iraq-Iran dispute, but could gather facts.
- IRAQI FOREIGN Minister Saadoun Hammadeh left here for New York to appear before the U.N. General Assembly and defend Iraq's position in the war, Baghdad Radio reported.
- In Washington, the State Department repeated assurances that the United States intends to remain neutral but said it opposes the seizure of territory by force by either Iraq or Iran.

According to reports, the Iraqis are moving troops, tanks, and armored personnel carriers southward toward the oil-rich Khuzestan province.

STRESSES DISARMAMENT:

Coffin speaks on military

By JULIE BROWN

Defending a nation is virtually impossible in a nuclear age, and striving for military superiority results in a weakening of security, a Presbyterian minister and social activist told more than 275 people at Rackham Auditorium last night.

"No longer are our weapons able to do what they were presumably intended to do," said William Sloane Coffin. Arms proliferation has made "the little man walking behind the president with an attache case obsolete," as experts estimate it would take Soviet missiles 30 minutes to reach the U.S., Coffin said.

COFFIN—ONE OF three clergymen allowed to visit the hostages in the American Embassy at Tehran last Christmas—spoke on "Disarmament, the Hostages, and the Campus." The lecture was sponsored by area churches and religious organizations.

Students must increase their awareness and understanding of the arms race, and then must pass this knowledge on to others, Coffin said.

The religious community has been active in opposing arms proliferation, and the intellectual community also has an obligation to educate individuals on the subject, the 56-year-old minister said.

COFFIN WAS THE chaplain at Yale University from 1958 to 1976, and has served for the last three years as senior minister at the Riverside Church in New York City. While at Yale, he was involved in anti-war activities, at one point offer-

See ACTIVIST, Page 5

...egent criticized in land deal resolution

...JAY McCORMACK

...aw County Democratic Party ... resolution criticizing University ... Roach (D-Saline) for supporting ... University land deal.

..., introduced by local Democrat ..., is in a committee and has not ... voted on by party members.

...—first brought by Pooley at an ... meeting and most recently ... week—chides Roach and the ...nts for approving an option for ... Stegeman to buy the lot on the ...view and S. Forest.

...OLD the Regents he planned to ... hotel-condominium-apartment ...site. At the February Regents ...troduced the motion to grant ...tion. The motion was narrowly ...board.

...veral groups and individuals have protested their decision. The project is currently awaiting action by the city Planning Commission.

Pooley said she first complained about the matter at the March Regents meeting. She said Roach did not welcome community comment. "I thought that Regent Roach dealt with us (those who protested the Regents' decision) all in a . . . paternalistic way."

POOLEY SAID SHE considered the treatment she had received in March over the summer, and decided to introduce a resolution concerning the matter at the August County party meeting.

Roach said the resolution was "unprecedented, in my view unwarranted, and naive. It's not the way it's done. I think it's a matter that will be resolved within the party."

Pooley's fellow party member Neil Staebler also said the matter was handled improperly. "The resolution was first brought up at a county meeting with no attempts to get the facts. I criticize it very vigorously on that ground."

"THE RESOLUTION got greater publicity than I had counted on," Pooley said. "I viewed it as an internal matter within the party. I did not view it as a formal move of censure." But she added that she thinks it is good that an individual can do something. "The system can be made responsive," she said.

The issue came up for discussion at last Thursday's party meeting. The resolution was read and Pooley, Roach, and other Democrats commented.

Staebler opposed Pooley at the meeting, and said in an interview last night that "the content—attacking a person rather than the board was an unfair way of producing it. I don't think she thought it through, but just dumped it in."

STAEBLER SAID HE opposes the building of the Stegeman project, disagreeing with Pooley only in the method of her attack of the problem.

Democratic Councilman Kenneth Latta (D-First Ward) said Pooley's grievances stemmed from a feeling of unhappiness among certain Democrats with Roach's performance on more than just the Stegeman deal. The running of a pro-Graduate Employees Organization student candidate against Roach in the regent's last campaign indicated one source of unease, said Latta. He added there are parts of the platform which Roach does not follow.

The measure will not come up for a party vote before November and at least one area Democrat is very skeptical about its chance for approval.

"It won't be passed," said second ward councilman Earl Greene.

Pooley said she is somewhat satisifed already. "I think I've achieved what I wanted in that the matter is being discussed." She added that bringing out such problems is a good thing in itself, "This is your view. You should put it forward and let the chips fall."

Roach
. . . under fire

TODAY

...ace and show

...SON SLITHERED across the finish line ... A lethargic Reagan, who tended to put his ...n his mouth in the heat of the race, came ...ond. And Carter, the creature with hand-... his belly came in last. That was the out-... as three resplendent reptiles named ..., and Anderson squared off for the first ...ympics in the tiny town of Lizard Lick, North ...izard trio was expected to hot-foot it down ...sand-covered tracks painted red, white and ...dn't exactly turn out that way. All three ...ble, but Anderson, with a blinding burst of ... through the first lap in no time at all. He ... almost choked on the second lap, though, ...efused to budge. Contestant Reagan clung ...the track's ceiling. Carter started to move, ... but Anderson recovered from his first burst of speed and crossed the finish line before his opponents. The candidates had little to say after the race was over, but Reagan's campaign manager was a little upset because the race was too much for the exhausted reptile. He uncurled his fingers to reveal an almost catotonic Regan and said sadly that his lizard was just too old. □

Early to bed

If you are one of those people who are late to bed and late to rise be glad you don't go to Yale. In an effort to conserve energy, Yale University is trying to roust students out of bed by offering popular courses early in the morning. Most college students stay up late at night and sleep in late, but a Yale study shows that if this habit could be changed energy consumption could be cut significantly. College Dean Howard Lamar changed his popular course called "History of the Trans-Mississippi West," also known as "Cowboys and Indians," to 8:30 a.m. to conform with the university's policy. "To my surprise it seems to be working," Lamar says. He notes that enrollment did not decline much from when it was offered later in the mornings. While early to bed, early to rise may not make Yalies healthy and wealthy, it may make them wise. □

Just funnin'

It was not as good as Orsen Welles' War of the Worlds stunt, but Tony Johnson of radio station WTRX in Flint wanted to liven up his show with a little pun. So he broke into his patter last week to say, "We have a bulletin. I just heard that a cement truck and a Flint police van carrying prisoners has just collided off Flint's east side. Be on the lookout for twelve 'hardened' criminals." Hardened criminals. Cement. Get it? Neither did parents in the area. They swamped area school switchboards with calls and forced the evacuation of two elementary schools until the criminals could be caught. □

You are what you wear

A recent survey by four researchers at the University of California found that teenage boys read more sexual connotations into girls' dress and behavior than most girls intend. While most teenage girls think that tight jeans and no bra is simply in vogue, adolescent guys view this type of dress as a sexual come-on. The survey of 432 young people, 14 to 18 years old, did find some agreement between the sexes on sexual signals. It was concluded that a girl in a see-through blouse was probably trying to come-on to her male counterparts. However, the dress of a male doesn't give his sexual interests away. According to the teens surveyed, just because a male wears an open shirt, tight pants or a low cut pair of swim trunks, his apparel is not a good indicator for females of his interests. □

On the inside

Sports provides a preview of the ...ad Ali-Larry Holmes match . . . Arts reviews the ... Ann Arbor Jazz Festival . . . and Howard ...ses his guilt over registering for the draft.

If you see news happen, call 76-DAILY

The Michigan Daily

Ann Arbor, Michigan — Monday, October 1, 1990

Touchdown
Jon Vaughn celebrates his touchdown in the first half of Saturday's game. The Wolverines defeated the Maryland Terrapins, 45-17.

House sends budget plan to Senate

WASHINGTON (AP) — President Bush and congressional leaders yesterday forged a $500 billion five-year compromise package of tax increases and spending cuts spurring Congress to quick action on a stop-gap spending measure needed to avoid cutbacks in federal services today.

The House approved the temporary financing bill just three hours after the budget agreement was described by President Bush in a Rose Garden announcement.

The Senate was poised to act later in the evening.

"It is balanced, it is fair, and in my view it is what the United States of America needs at this point in its history," Bush said in announcing an agreement that concluded budget negotiations that began in May.

The package contained $134 billion in new tax revenues, including new taxes on gasoline, cigarettes, alcohol and luxury items. Medicare costs for the elderly and disabled were increased, defense spending was slashed as well.

The House passed what is called a continuing appropriations resolution to keep the government operating at full speed through next Friday while lawmakers weigh the proposed budget compromise.

The resolution sent quickly to the Senate also includes $2 billion in new appropriations for the Desert Shield operations in the Persian Gulf.

House Speaker Thomas Foley (D-Wash.) praised the compromise, but agreed with Senate Democratic leader George Mitchell (Maine) who said, "Now comes the hard part," in pushing it past special interest groups and through Congress.

The compromise would shear $40 billion off the deficit expected for the new fiscal year. Without action, the 1991 shortfall was projected to hit $294 billion, $73 billion higher than the previous federal record for red ink and almost triple the shortfall the administration said it anticipated in January.

White House budget director Richard Darman attributed the higher deficit projection to the deteriorating economy and growing projections of the costs of rescuing the savings and loan industry.

"It's going to be very painful for a lot of people," said Dole, "predicting a tough fight for enough votes to get the agreement past Congress."

bars, liquor stores confiscate fake IDs

...campus are becoming [fake] IDs are getting better, and liquor retailers have never fake IDs since [the incident]..., general manager of "On a busy weekend five to six people have..."

...cause their IDs just don't look right; two years ago it was double that." Their strict policy of accepting only drivers' licenses and passports as IDs keeps people from trying, said Stadler.

Checkers know what to look for on out-of-state licenses by comparing them to those in a book which shows all licenses in the country. Often times, the picture, expiration date, signature, or lamination are clues to checkers that the ID is counterfeit.

"Most often we see people borrowing legitimate IDs from their friends, we catch them by checking the picture closely and by asking them what their zip code or zodiac sign is," Stadler said.

Jack Weinmann, Village Corner Party Store personnel manager, has also seen a decline in the number of fake IDs. "Before we started prosecuting two years ago, we would see 10 to 15 IDs on a Friday night, now we collect 10 to 15 a month," he said. Weinmann attributed the decline to the store's policy of turning fake IDs over to the police.

"We know what practically every ID in the country looks like," he said. "Because of extra enforcement of liquor laws, retailers have to be extremely careful."

The Quality Bar also has a policy of confiscating IDs, said Beth Reibel, assistant manager. "The number of fake IDs we get on a busy night varies radically, but there is a definite increase when the students are in town."

One to seven fake IDs are confiscated on
See FAKE, Page 2

drafted for [de]velopment [ea]st Detroit

...new proposal of Detroit's build a new ...er all ...wo police de-with manda-...dollar plan, developers and Michigan e Walbridge firm, has yet [the] city. A pre-drafted by [said] in Detroit's was obtained [f]or a report in...

...ney, about [vested] in an area [ab]andoned and [w]ould foster [ters]...in an at-...prostitution,

...pornography, gambling and other criminal activities," the proposal says.

The new town would be home to about 7,500 people of mixed races and income levels. It would have a semi-autonomous government with authority to control its own development and social programs.

The community would have a separate police department, but the plan did not specify how Detroit would be involved in the hiring or running of the force. It would also have its own school district that would require drug tests and weapons searches.

The plan calls for Detroit to demolish buildings, relocate residents, clean up environmental hazards and relocate roads and utilities. When that is completed, the developers want the city to hand over the property.

See DETROIT, Page 2

Hispanic heritage
The Mexican dance group Los Hijos de Aztlan performs at the Latino Arts Extravaganza Friday in the Pendleton Room of the Union.

Saddam requests peaceful discourse

by the Associated Press

Saddam Hussein adopted a more conciliatory stance yesterday in the nearly 2-month-old Persian Gulf crisis, urging peaceful dialogue instead of "threats and warnings."

In a message broadcast on Iraqi TV and radio, Saddam also said he no longer opposed the involvement of foreign powers in the search for a settlement to the crisis, which was touched off by Iraq's Aug. 2 invasion of Kuwait.

Saddam's speech, read by an announcer, said tensions can be reduced in the gulf "if dialogue replaces the policy of threats and warnings, if the language of peaceful politics replaces the policy of troop buildups and threats of the use of force."

"Peace could not be achieved without the settlement of all the problems of the region," he said.

European and Israeli military analysts say there is still a window for peace, before the effects of sanctions sink in further and U.S.-led forces in Saudi Arabia become strong enough to consider launching a military operation to push Iraq out of Kuwait.

"I think another six to eight weeks is available to prevent a conflict, but after that it becomes almost inevitable," said Paul Beaver, publisher of Jane's Defense Weekly.

With the United Nations demanding an unconditional Iraqi withdrawal from Kuwait and Iraqi reiterating almost daily that it will not retreat, the analysts see little room for a negotiated solution.

"Saddam Hussein could well now be driven into a corner which makes negotiations difficult and we could see a situation where he is left with few options and those all being of a military nature," Beaver said in an interview.

See SADDAM, Page 2

[Demo]crats seek to bag 'user-fee' proposal

...at the Republican Caucus last night.
"I have trouble supporting major cuts in mid-fiscal year," said councilmember Jerry Schleicher (R-4th Ward).

"I think the proposal is very political and downright stupid," councilmember Ingrid Sheldon (R-2nd Ward). "It is very unfair on graded cuts to help [reduce the] deficit in...

The proposed user-fee would have charged households a $1 pick-up fee for each additional bag or can after the first 35-gallon can. According to several landlords, such an increase [would] have resulted in higher rents [on] fall.

Mike Garfield, environmental issues coordinator at Ann Arbor's Ecology Center, said, "I support the...

...(the city council's recent) proposal was not thought out that well." He added he didn't think the proposal was designed to encourage recycling but rather to raise money to cover the Solid Waste department's deficit.

The department needs the extra revenue to make up for a $1.7 million deficit. Increasing costs for collecting the city's trash and rising costs of [...]

City, unions react to garbage privatization
by Donna Woodwell
Daily City Reporter

Since the city council passed a resolution Sept. 17 allowing the city to put its contracts for solid waste up for private bid, city officials and union workers have been pondering the ramifications.

Thais Anne Peterson (D-5th Ward), the only council member to oppose the resolution, disagreed with it for several reasons. "I'm not sure the bottom line shows all," she said.

"If we privatize, then I lose my ability to control how we handle our waste," Peterson said. "I don't like the notion of transferring (the city's waste disposal) capital to private companies because that would not change our minds."

transport and dumping at the Browning-Ferris Industries (BFI) landfill in Salem Township account for much of the deficit.

The city's own landfill is full and currently undergoing expansion financed by $28 million raised in a bond issue vote last April. These funds are earmarked for cleaning up the city's landfill, construction of a recycling plant and monthly curbside pick-ups and do not cover increases in solid waste disposal costs.

The city's budget is determined in April. Any changes made to the budget needs eight city council votes to pass.

According to the resolution, "significant cost savings... may be possible through the use of private contractors." However, councilmember Jerry Schleicher (R-4th Ward) said the exact amount of savings is still being studied, and will not be known until the bids are returned on Nov. 15.

See GARBAGE, page 2

1990

You can see in the 1990 cover of *The Michigan Daily* a partial return to the grid, along with the first clear design demarcation dividing above and below the fold.* Both the top segment and the bottom segment align to a six column grid and use slightly different sizes of the same headline format. The top and the bottom are separated by a long, thin story strip, which creates a divide between the top half of the page (above the fold) and the bottom half (below the fold). This strip breaks the grid and uses five thicker columns which do not line up with the rest of the page. Photographs are getting bigger and stories are less condensed on the page, taking up less vertical and more rectangular segments of the paper.

---

* The fold references the center point of the front page, which folds in half. Above the fold is the content that is visable from the top, and below the fold is the bottom half of the page that folds under.

2000

The 2000 cover of *The Michigan Daily* is the first example of a color copy of the front page. The rule that separates the masthead from the headline is now blue, along with color photography and red and blue rules at the bottom of the page. This is also the first example of a story set-up called the 'C' format. This format consists of five stories that are oriented in a 'C' shape, with the first starting on the far right side (titled "Court proceedings..."), then moving accross to the left ("Larceny drops..."), down to the bottom left, than back over to the bottom right. There is also the addition of a bottom tease, the long thin column at the bottom of the page which is teasing to stories from different sections Inside.

The Michigan Daily

One hundred ten years of editorial freedom

Thursday
December 7, 2000

Battle returns to Fla. high court

Richard Barrazza holds a sign with his holiday wish during a rally in support of Texas Gov. George W. Bush yesterday in El Paso, Texas. About 50 Bush supporters gathered for the rally.

Court proceedings moving at rapid pace

TALLAHASSEE, Fla. (AP) — Al Gore hung his presidential hopes on legal proceedings moving at head-spinning speed a day ahead of arguments before the Florida Supreme Court, counting on a court shocker to upset George W. Bush's certified Florida victory.

Lawyers sprinted between courtrooms yesterday to battle over absentee ballots while Bush and Gore submitted papers to persuade the state Supreme Court to rule their way in a fight over recounts.

Late in the day, Republican legislative leaders called for a special session on Friday to choose a slate of electors. The two leaders said they hoped such a step wouldn't be needed if there's a court resolution of the disputed election.

Democrats denounced the action as a mistake of historic proportions, and accused GOP rivals of moving to ensure Bush's election.

"We're protecting Florida's 25 electoral votes and its 6 million voters," said John McKay, the president of the state Senate.

Rep. Lois Frankel, leader of the House Democrats, shot back, "The only thing missing on the proclamation is the postmark from Austin, Texas," a reference to the Texas governor's campaign headquarters.

Gore's team set the stakes in its filing with the high court, writing: "In but a few more days, only the judgment of history will be left to fall upon a system where deliberate obstruction has succeeded in achieving delay and where further delays risk succeeding in handing democracy a defeat."

Bush's team countered that the people had spoken on Election Day and that "at no time in our nation's history has a presidential race been decided by an election contest in a court of law."

The stalemate that has loomed since Nov. 7 seemed to be nearing the end of overtime and heading to a sudden-death score, almost surely in the form of a court ruling.

One surprise might come from two parallel cases unfolding before separate judges in the same Tallahassee courthouse.

Democrats were challenging a total of 25,000 absentee ballots in Seminole and Martin counties, saying Republicans had been unfairly permitted to correct mistakes on ballot applications, in violation of state law.

Either suit had the potential to switch the lead in Florida's vote count from Bush to Gore, since Bush won the absentee ballots by a 2-to-1 margin.

Bush, leading by a few hundred votes ever since the Nov. 7 election and talking more like a president-elect each day, said he had "pretty well made up my mind" on his White House

See RECOUNT, Page 7A

Larceny drops on campus

By David Enders
Daily Staff Reporter

The holiday season traditionally brings a rise in larcenies, but a look back at the last six months shows that overall larceny on campus has dropped for the same period last year, according to Department of Public Safety statistics.

DPS perennially identifies the Central Recreation Building and Intramural Sports Building, the University's Hospitals and libraries as the most common sites of theft, while overall incidents of larceny are down, theft at the CCRB and the IM Building rose.

Three hundred and forty-one larcenies from a building were reported from September to November 1999, compared to 294 for the same period this year, according to DPS statistics. For the CCRB, there were 23 incidences of theft compared to 10 last year. At the IM, theft rose from zero to seven incidences.

DPS attributes the thefts to patrons leaving gym bags unattended. "I think it's helpful for people to know theft are lockers — they cost a quarter, but when you're done, you get the quarter back," Brown said.

Brown said DPS officers suspect thieves simply come into the CCRB and leave unnoticed with a bag that is not theirs. "They're coming in dressed like everyone else in basketball clothes and sweats, and they blend in with the crowd," she said. "Our theft is not students. It's people coming from the outside."

Associate Director of Recreational Sports Deborah Webb said the CCRB takes precautions to keep non-affiliates of the University from coming into the CCRB.

"We've got people stationed at the entries and swiping MCards," Webb said. "So I don't know that people who are stealing don't have a University affiliation."

Webb said that students should use the lockers and avoid an "it won't happen to me" attitude about theft.

"They play basketball and think they can keep an eye on their bag," she said.

"Backpack thieves in the libraries work much the same way.

"We are very aware, especially at this time of the year that we are more theft," said Brenda Johnson, the associate director for public services in the University Library System. "In the evening, we have security monitors who walk around the building," she said. "After midnight, at the Shapiro (Undergraduate Library) you have to be a U of M student" to enter.

Brown also warned against two other kinds of thefts common during this time of year.

"Credit card theft rises nationwide at the holidays," she said, also mentioning another crime students may not often consider.

"As we approach the back buyback season, we see an increase in textbook thefts," Brown said. "It's very frustrating because that's when everyone needs them to study for their exams."

A student leaves his coat unattended in the locker room of the CCRB. DPS statistics show that while crime is down overall on campus, larceny is up at the CCRB.

Students in APA discuss diversity

By Anna Clark
Daily Staff Reporter

By being paired with whites in the University's admissions policies, Asian American students are not beneficiaries of affirmative action. But almost three years after the filing of two lawsuits challenging the race-based admissions policies in the College of Literature, Science and the Arts and the Law School, campus groups representing Asian cultures still haven't taken an official position on the issue.

That will change next week when University Asian Organizations, the umbrella group for Asian student organizations at the University, will vote on a stance.

To preface the vote, the Asian Pacific Association hosted an affirmative action debate at their regular meeting last night in a South Quad multicultural lounge.

Law third-year students Amit Kurlekar and Ryan Wu presented opposing arguments before a group of about 40 University students and staff members, some of whom are not part of APA but were drawn to the event out of personal interest.

LSA senior Avani Sheth, moderator of the debate and UAO advocacy chair, said the event was intended to primarily be educational.

Asian Pacific students "tend to be an excluded voice on political issues on

See ASIAN AMERICANS, Page 7A

'U' symposium debates use of 'CopyRIGHTS'

By Maria Sprow
Daily Staff Reporter

The University's use of 'CopyRIGHTS' provided material for debate during the last day of the University's symposium on the legal provisions involved in copyrighting.

The panel discussion featured speakers James Hilton, a professor of psychology; Roberta Morris, an Law School adjunct professor, Jonathan Alger, the assistant general council to the University, Chief Information Officer Jose-Marie Griffiths and William Gosling, the director of the University library.

The panel discussed fair use rights, the University's support of copyrighted material in the classroom and faculty produced scholarly material.

Faculty and staff, during a discussion, addressed the need for guidelines regarding copyrighted material. Responding defensively, Information Prof. Victor Rosenberg compared the University's stance on copyright issues to that on affirmative action.

Rosenberg stated the University has not changed its policies regarding affirmative action in the face of the threat of public disapproval and asked why the University isn't

See COPYRIGHTS, Page 7A

Duke opens chapel to same-sex unions

By Rachel Green
Daily Staff Reporter

Duke University announced yesterday its decision to open the university's chapel to same-sex union ceremonies.

A student government proposal prompted the decision. University President Nannerl Keohane and Dean of Chapel William Willimon, signed the agreement that permits same-sex unions for all students, faculty and staff affiliated with the university, provided the couple's denomination supports same-sex unions.

John Burness, a spokesman for the university, said the unions are protected under the university's non-discrimination policy.

"This policy does not and cannot discriminate based on sexual orientation," Burness said.

Founded in conjunction with the United Methodist Church, Duke has become the fifth private university in the country to recognize such unions, following the lead of Harvard, Stanford, Emory and Wake Forest.

Burness said the role of the Methodist church has changed significantly over the course of the long-standing relationship between the church and university.

"While the seminary is still a Methodist seminary, the Duke chapel is not itself affiliated with the Methodist church," Burness said. "The Duke chapel is a Duke building — a public building."

Karen Krahulik, director of Duke's center for lesbian, gay, bisexual and transgender life, said she believes student activism was the main reason

See DUKE, Page 2A

LSA sophomores Zach Schulman and Marjorie Rodes and LSA freshman Catherine Ellingson talk last night at a candle light vigil sponsored by SOLE on the steps of the Michigan Union.

WEATHER
27°
Snow
Tonight: Snow. Low 18.
Tomorrow: Foggy. High 34.

NEWS
SOLE holds candlelight vigil
Students Organizing for Labor Equality hold a candlelight vigil in memory of those killed by a fire in a Bangladeshi textile factory. **PAGE 3A.**

WEEKEND, ETC.
Happy holidays
Weekend, Etc. counts down the best holiday movies, interviews the big elf himself and takes a look at alternative holiday plans. **PAGE 1B.**

SPORTS
Wrestling the Spartans
The Michigan wrestling team takes on Michigan State for intrastate dominance this weekend. **PAGE 5A.**

THE BIG CHILL — The Daily previews the outdoor event that will likely break hockey attendance records. »INSIDE

A WORTHY OPPONENT — Michigan takes on Akron, which beat the Wolverines 7-1 in October, tonight in the NCAA semifinals. »PAGE 8A

The Michigan Daily

ONE HUNDRED TWENTY-ONE YEARS OF EDITORIAL FREEDOM

Ann Arbor, Michigan — Friday, December 10, 2010 — michigandaily.com

ENGINEERING THE P-P-P-PERFECT P-P-P-POKER FACE

For a full story on the Mr. Engineer pageant visit the Daily's News blog at michigandaily.com/blogs/The Wire.

Engineering senior Andrew Gavenda sings Lady Gaga's hit song "Poker Face" for the talent portion of the Mr. Engineer contest in Stamps Auditorium yesterday. Michigan Student Assembly President Chris Armstrong and Engineering Dean David Munson judged the competition.
CHRIS RYBA/Daily

OPEN HOUSING INITIATIVE

With letter, ACLU makes push for open housing plan

Proposal is 'critical to ensuring equal rights,' letter says

By CLAIRE GOSCICKI
Daily Staff Reporter

The University's chapter of the American Civil Liberties Union sent a letter to University Housing administrators this week urging them to enact the Open Housing Initiative, a proposal designed by members of the Michigan Student Assembly and other student groups that would offer students living in University residences the option of choosing a roommate of any gender.

The letter states that implementation of the initiative is "critical to ensuring equal rights for all students living in residence halls," and that "adapting housing policy to include an open housing option is consistent with the University's commitment to non-discrimination."

The Washtenaw County and state of Michigan ACLU branches also expressed support for gender-neutral University housing by signing the letter.

The Open Housing Initiative submitted a report months in the making to University Housing officials last month, urging the body to offer a gender-neutral housing option starting in the fall. The day after the students submitted the proposal, Director of University Housing Linda Newman said it was unlikely that the proposal would be implemented come fall.

"Typically we always do the room sign-up for returning students in late January," Newman told the Daily at the time. "Before people sign up, we have a marketing period where we let people know what to expect, what we're offering."

LSA senior Mallory Jones, chair of the University's chapter of the ACLU and a former news editor for the Daily, called the initiative a "good, progressive policy," adding that it's important because it would ensure that all students have equal access to University Housing.

"As the ACLU, we feel that the implementation of an open housing policy is critical to ensuring equal rights for all students living in residence halls, including transgender students," the letter states. "The cur-
See ACLU, Page 3A

BIG CHILL AT THE BIG HOUSE

Students criticize assigned seating scheme for Big Chill

Originally, policy allowed for general admission in student section

By JOSEPH LICHTERMAN
Daily Staff Reporter

Though this Saturday's Big Chill at the Big House is sold out, some students aren't pleased about a change in the student ticket policy for the outdoor hockey game at Michigan Stadium between the Wolverines and Michigan State University.

When officials first announced the Big Chill last January, the Athletic Department initially planned on having the student section — located in sections 25-32 in the northwest corner of the stadium — be a general admissions area. However, after experiencing problems with general admission seating at the Big House for Spring Commencement in May, the Athletic Department changed its policy, according to Athletic Department spokesman David Ablauf.

"At graduation, it became very obvious that people would not fill the sections to capacity and there was concern from a security standpoint about getting all students adequately seated," Ablauf wrote in an e-mail.

Tickets to the game were included in both football and hockey student season ticket packages for $5. Students were also able to purchase additional tickets for $10 each.

In March, when the initial e-mail about purchasing tickets was sent to students, the Athletic Department intended to allow
See TICKETS, Page 3A

IMMIGRATION POLICY

'U' supporters are cautiously optimistic about DREAM vote

After measure clears House, bill still faces uphill battle in Senate

By SUZANNE JACOBS
Daily Staff Reporter

In a victorious late-term push by the lame duck Democratic majority, the U.S. House of Representatives passed a bill Wednesday that would grant temporary legal status to hundreds of thousands of undocumented students, and give them the opportunity to gain permanent resident status.

First introduced to the U.S. Senate in 2001, the Development, Relief and Education for Alien Minors Act — commonly known as the DREAM Act — would allow six-year permanent resident status to individuals who came to the U.S. before turning 16, have graduated from high school or obtained a GED certificate, are under the age of 35, demonstrate "good moral character" and have lived in the U.S. for at least five consecutive years at the time of the bill's enactment.

After completing at least two years of higher education or military service, these individuals would be able to apply for five more years of non-immigrant status, and after ten years, they would be eligible to apply for permanent residency.

Though supporters both in Congress and at the University say they are optimistic about Wednesday's vote, they said the fight to turn the bill into law is far from over.

Sociology Prof. Silvia Pedraza said she watched the vote on the bill on C-Span and was happy
See DREAM, Page 3A

NOT YOUR AVERAGE RELATIONSHIP STATUS

Student-run dance crews like Dance 2XS, which told the story of two Facebook lovers, competed in the second annual Michigan's Best Dance Crew competition at the Michigan League last night. Funktion ultimately won the competition.
TODD NEEDLE/Daily

ALUMNI AND THE COMMUNITY

In mentor program, 'U' alumni help high school students plan for college

Michigan College Advising Corps places graduates in schools across state

By ROBIN VEECK
Daily Staff Reporter

Though University alum Joilyn Stephenson signed up for the Michigan College Advising Corps to help give low-income high school students the tools to apply to and attend colleges like the University, after a few months working at Pontiac High School, she says the students have had an impact on her as well.

"Some of these students come from a difficult background, but they still have it in their heart to make the most out of their future," Stephenson wrote in an e-mail interview. "That in itself is amazing."

Stephenson is one of eight recent University graduates currently working in Michigan public schools to help students from underserved districts apply to and attend college.

Each adviser in the program, which the University launched in April, works full-time in a school with traditionally low college matriculation rates.

Christopher Rutherford, College Advising Corps program manager at the Center for Educational Outreach, said the program has four primary goals.

"Those goals are first centered around increasing the number of students that go on to four-year institutions," Rutherford said. "The second goal is to increase the types
See CORPS, Page 3A

GETTING AROUND THE CITY

Cabbies say Ann Arbor a prime market

Low barriers to entry, large student body help many companies profit

By ADAM RUBENFIRE
Daily Staff Reporter

According to frequent cab riders, a cab company official and the self-proclaimed "King of the Cabbies," Ann Arbor is a prime place for the taxi business.

Area cab aficionados say the combination of a large population of students — both sober and drunk — and a relatively accessible licensing process has created somewhat of an oasis for taxicabs in an area of the country well known for its reliance on private vehicles.

According to Ann Arbor Police Officer Bill Clock, who works in AAPD's Special Services Unit and is responsible for the licensing of taxis and their drivers, there are currently 166 licensed taxicabs in the city, as well as 310 licensed drivers.

In addition to the high volume of taxicabs, Clock said he's seen a recent increase in limousines for hire, which operate on a flat rate instead of a meter.

James Fowler, assistant to the owner of Blue Cab, said Ann Arbor's taxicab scene is especially vibrant for a place like southeast Michigan.

"There's a population of about 120,000, plus another 80,000 kids," Fowler said. "It's a good market; (but) it's a great market for this area."

Blue Cab has approximately 50 drivers for its fleet of about 40
See TAXIS, Page 3A

38

WEATHER TOMORROW HI: 36 LO: 30

GOT A NEWS TIP? Call 734-763-2459 or e-mail news@michigandaily.com and let us know.

NEW ON MICHIGANDAILY.COM Adventures Abroad: Reflections from London. MICHIGANDAILY.COM/BLOGS/THE WIRE

INDEX Vol. CXXI, No. 64 ©2010 The Michigan Daily michigandaily.com

NEWS.........2A CLASSIFIEDS......6A
OPINION......4A SPORTS..........7A
ARTS..........5A THE BIG CHILL....1B

2010

In 2010 *The Michigan Daily* returned to a streamlined grid layout. As you can see, every story aligns to the same six columns. The story format is still the same 'C' shaped design that we saw in 2000, only now there are small blue labels above the headlines which group the stories into genres. This label, called a kicker,* is in a condensed sans serif font that visually connects the stories together while letting the reader know the general theme of the piece. This is also the first example of a rule explicitly dividing the top and bottom half of the page, creating a visible division. You will also notice that the bottom tease from 2000 has been moved to the top of the page, above the masthead, and has expanded from only textual cues to using illustrated graphic elements, as well.

* Words above the article that are generally set in a different type face, that organize the articles by categorizing them into broader genres.

2015

The Michigan Daily maintained the story layout from 2010, but made some subtle adjustments in an attempt to modernize it. The photograph is more consistently paired with story two in the upper left-hand corner, and spreads across four of the six columns. The second photograph, below the fold on the right, has a rule dividing it on all sides, with a caption above it, reading "Spider-woman." This is an example of a feature photo,* which gives the reader a sneak peak at a story inside. It adds a visual element to a front page when there is no photo coverage of the events in the cover stories. The teaser to the inside has been moved from above the masthead back to the bottom, like the 2000 cover. However, this time it is almost entirely graphic.

---

* A photograph that is placed on the front page but is separate from the front page stories. It often is a high quality photo from a story inside the paper which was placed on the front for its visual appeal.

The Michigan Daily

ONE HUNDRED AND TWENTY FIVE YEARS OF EDITORIAL FREEDOM

Ann Arbor, Michigan | Wednesday, September 30, 2015 | michigandaily.com

First-year Law student Shirin Makhkamova sets out candles over the block 'M' on the Diag to honor lives lost and in peril in the Syrian refugee crisis on Tuesday.
RITA MORRIS/Daily

Student groups organize vigil for Syrian refugees

Speakers focus on humanizing those affected by the crisis

By TANYA MADHANI
Daily Staff Reporter

University students and Ann Arbor residents gathered on the Diag on Tuesday at a vigil for Syrian refugees.

The University's Muslim Graduate Students Association and Muslim Law Students Association held the vigil to honor Syrian refugees who lost their lives and those who are still struggling to reach a safety. The flood of Syrian refugees into Europe has sparked debate in recent weeks as world leaders struggle with how to handle the influx of people fleeing unrest in their home country.

Third-year law student Omar El-Halwagi, co-president of MLSA, said he and the president of MGSA decided to hold the vigil to call attention to issues impacting Muslims globally.

"There is no greater human rights crisis right now than the Syrian refugee (crisis) and we're all watching it unfold," El-Halwagi said. "We've been watching it unfold for years. We finally felt there was enough momentum to get something done."

El-Halwagi said he hopes students become better informed on the issue so that it will be more likely they will take action in the future.

"We have the next generation of leaders attending this school and they need to be able to be aware of what's going on," he said. "I also think college campuses are really ripe for activism and advocacy. By being able to put on
See **VIGIL**, Page 3A

CAMPUS CONTEXT

One year in, Schlissel says diversity plan moves ahead

President slated to roll out strategic initiative on inclusion by spring 2016

By EMMA KINERY
Daily Staff Reporter

University President Mark Schlissel and his administration have spent the last academic year working to roll out new policy initiatives regarding several campus issues — most notably athletics, diversity, alcohol abuse and Greek life. This week, the *Michigan Daily* reviews the events that got the ball rolling. Today, we consider Schlissel's work to address campus diversity, namely through the gradual unveiling of his administration's strategic campus plan to be released by the end of this year.

The overview: Diversity has long been a battle-tested issue at the University. Currently, minority enrollment lies at 11.53 percent — and in recent years, students have continually lobbied the University to make the campus more welcoming to minority students, both in terms of social climate and admissions.

The changes: University President Mark Schlissel has worked to address the school's apparent lack of diversity by introducing a campus-wide strategic plan, which he will unveil at the end of this school year (also the end of his second year in office). Most recently, this has included launching the HAIL Scholarship, which offers full-ride tuition for high-achieving, low-income students. Initiatives through the Office of Student Life have also sought to heavily incorporate students in catalyzing culture shift at the University.
See **SCHLISSEL**, Page 3A

ACADEMICS

'U' alum given MacArthur for research about ancient Greece

Dimitri Nakassis wins $650,000 to pursue study focused on classics

By TANYA MADHANI
Daily Staff Reporter

In the fall of 1993, then-LSA freshman Dimitri Nakassis was flipping through a course pack to decide which classes he wanted to take when he stumbled upon two courses that piqued his interest: Introduction to Field Archeology, and Intro to Greek Art and Architecture.

Twenty-two years later, Nakassis' research on Mycenaean Greek society — which represents the last phase of the Bronze Age in Ancient Greece — and the relationship between its nobility and working class earned him the 2015 MacArthur Fellowship. He is one of 24 individuals to receive the fellowship, a stipend of $625,000 that is often referred to as the "genius grant." This year's winners also include Atlantic correspondent Ta Nehisi-Coates and playwright and actor Lin Manuel Miranda.

"It's part of a bigger project of trying to understand Mycenae society, not just by looking at the people in the palace and not just looking at the palace, but also by looking at what's happening outside the palace," he said. "So, if you wanted to understand Ann Arbor, you couldn't just look at the University campus, right?"

Much of Nakassis's study is dedicated to researching ancient Greek linear tablets, which are scripts that recorded the earliest form of the Greek language. The tablets are administrative palatial documents that note the events at the palace and the individuals present.

"Like a lot of students, I wasn't really sure what to major in," Nakassis said. "Initially my plan was to double major or have a double concentration in history or economics. I was in my room at Markley and I was
See **GENIUS**, Page 3A

SPIDER-WOMAN

LSA senior Aubrey O'Neal scales the side of the School of Dentistry during Michigan Parkour practice on Tuesday.
EMILIE FARRUGIA/Daily

RESEARCH

Small interventions shown to decrease youth drinking

Study says emergency room talks could change risky behavior

By LYDIA MURRAY
For the Daily

The results of a recently released five-year trial from the University of Michigan Injury Center discovered that short interventions by hospital staff or computer programs correlated with decreases in underage alcohol consumption.

Patients ages 14-20 admitted to the emergency department were asked to report on their drinking behaviors, and researchers evaluated whether or not their behaviors were considered risky.

Those whom researchers found to be "risky drinkers" were then randomly assigned to receive a short intervention by means of a therapist or a computer program.

Associate Psychiatry Prof. Maureen Walton, one of the study's lead authors, outlined the research metrics:

"We asked them three questions about how many drinks per week they have and how many days per week that they drink, See **EMERGENCY**, Page 3A

HIGHER EDUCATION

Coleman appointed next AAU president

President emerita to lead association of 62 research universities

By SAM GRINGLAS
Managing News Editor

University President Emerita Mary Sue Coleman has been named president of the Association of American Universities.

The appointment is effective June 1. Coleman succeeds Hunter Rawlings III, who led the organization since 2011 and announced his plans to retire from the post in May.

"Hunter Rawlings has done an exceptional job as AAU president in advancing our collective impact as research institutions," Coleman wrote in a statement. "I am eager to continue the work of elevating the American research university as essential to our nation's prosperity, security, and well-being."
See **COLEMAN**, Page 3A

THE STATEMENT
A look at the Greek life crisis

INSIDE 41

| WEATHER TOMORROW | HI: 63 LO: 41 | GOT A NEWS TIP? Call 734-418-4115 or e-mail news@michigandaily.com and let us know. | NEW ON MICHIGANDAILY.COM TMD celebrates 125 years EDITOR'S BLOG | INDEX Vol. CXXV, No. 1 ©2015 The Michigan Daily michigandaily.com | NEWS..........2A OPINION......4A ARTS...........5A | SPORTS........7A CLASSIFIEDS...6A THE STATEMENT...1B |

REDESIGN

The Michigan Daily unveiled a complete redesign at the beginning of the 2016-2017 academic year. For the redesign, we looked both at the past iterations of the *Daily* and current trends in digital platforms for inspiration. A trend that we saw on news websites is a photo-based blurb format* for stories at the top of the page, allowing the viewer access to multiple topics depending on interest. We sought to channel a similar form for print in our new tease section, which we brought from the bottom of the page to directly below the masthead. Its placement above the fold gave the reader a more immediate view of the story options, while the photos created a cleaner visual aesthetic. If you compare the first and second cover you can see that the number of photos used in the tease is flexible depending on the stories we want to feature each day. Additionally, each element in the new design is modular, and can be moved to accomodate special feature stories, as you can see in the third and fourth cover example. Typographically, we streamlined the headline fonts, making them bolder and uniform throughout the page. Our overall goal was to simplify the number of visual components and make a system that allowed for greater visual variety.

---

* A style adopted by online sources for magazines where photographs preview stories on the home page. They are often arranged in a grid format. The stories can be read by clicking on the photographs.

The Michigan Daily

ONE HUNDRED AND TWENTY-FIVE YEARS OF EDITORIAL FREEDOM

Ann Arbor, Michigan — Tuesday, September 6, 2016 — michigandaily.com

Over the Rainbow
The No. 7 Michigan football team returned to the Big House for the 2016 season with a 63-3 drubbing of an overmatched Hawaii team on Saturday.
» Page 1B

Members of the University of Michigan football team celebrate with students after defeating Hawaii, 63-3.
AMANDA ALLEN/Daily

Wolverines Steamroll Rainbow Warriors, 63-3, in season opener

Michigan cruises behind new starting quarterback and stellar defensive play

JACOB GASE
Daily Sports Editor

After intercepting Wilton Speight's first pass as the starting quarterback for the

Michigan football team, Hawaii briefly challenged the prevailing notion that they were about to be on the receiving end of a blowout at Michigan Stadium.

Rainbow Warriors, that notion was quickly reaffirmed when they promptly lost seven yards and punted the ball four plays later.

Moving backwards would

become a recurring theme of the game for Hawaii, which had an abysmal negative-17 total yards at the end of the first quarter and needed a strong second half

See **FOOTBALL**, Page 8A

GOVERNMENT
Mich. visit gives Trump new chance for outreach

In first visit to African-American church, candidate aims to shift tone

CAITLIN REEDY
Daily Staff Reporter

Republican presidential nominee Donald Trump visited a Black church Saturday in Detroit in an outreach attempt to the African-American community. Bishop Wayne T. Jackson, the Great Faith Ministries International congregation leader, hosted Trump and sat down with the candidate for a one-on-one interview with him.

The New York Times reported this visit as Trump's first as a presidential candidate to an African-American church. He visited with church members and did an interview with Jackson, which was not open to press. Trump called it an "amazing interview" on Twitter Saturday and complimented Jackson on his interviewing skills, going so far as to say they were "better than the people who are doing that

See **TRUMP**, Page 2A

LOCAL
City plans to initiate audit of A² police dept.

Ann Arbor manager aims to have contract in place by December

BRIAN KUANG
Daily Staff Reporter

Ten months after the city Human Rights Commission published a 42-page report calling for an independent audit of the Ann Arbor Police Department, the city manager's office has started taking the initial steps toward meeting the HRC's recommendations.

The report called for a review of department practices as well as the creation of a civilian-run police oversight board. It was created in wake of a community push for police oversight reform of the 2014 shooting death of Ann Arbor resident Aura Rosser, a Black woman, by an AAPD officer.

Different recommendations will follow different timelines. In a memo released on Aug. 31, City Manager Howard Lazarus released a tentative plan for hiring a police auditor, who would conduct an audit of the AAPD's internal review protocols and communicate the results.

Under Lazarus's timetable, the request for contracting an auditor would be written with community input and released by the end of October. The auditor would be contracted by the end of December with City Council approval. Once

See **POLICE**, Page 3A

Bill Clinton campaigns for Hillary Clinton in Detroit Labor Day parade

The former President marched alonside UAW union members Monday

LYDIA MURRAY
Daily Staff Reporter

Former President Bill Clinton joined United Auto Workers union members and others for the annual Detroit Labor Day Parade Monday morning aiming to demonstrate the Hillary Clinton campaign's commitment to working families.

The parade began at 9:30 a.m. and marched down Michigan Avenue. Bill Clinton marched, but did not speak during the event which drew thousands of union workers and other prominent state Democrats. The annual parade in Detroit has drawn important Democratic figures in the past, including President Barack Obama in 2008 and Vice President Joe Biden 2012 and 2014.

The parade's theme was "Your Vote is Your Voice and was dedicated to supporting working families and improving unions, as well as encouraging voter registration.

LSA junior Collin Kelly, chair of the University's chapter of College Democrats, said Bill Clinton's visit demonstrates that Hillary Clinton is the candidate who will best represent the interests of the working class.

"Bill Clinton coming to Detroit on Labor Day signifies the commitment of both the Democratic Party and the Clinton family to honoring, protecting and fighting for workers across the nation," he said. "Unions built this

country, but only Democrats seem to remember that. Bill Clinton knows that unions are part of why America is great, and he understands they are indispensable for our future."

Clinton's appearance was one of several similar events held by surrogates for his wife's campaign Monday: Hillary Clinton, along with running mate Sen. Tim Kaine (D-Va.) and Biden, hosted events in other Rust Belt areas such as Cleveland and Pittsburgh.

In a statement released Monday morning, Hillary

Clinton emphasized her commitment to workers in Michigan, citing her support for the auto industry and criticizing her opponent Donald Trump, stating that his policies would only harm the middle class.

"Don't let anyone tell you we can't 'Make it in America' anymore," Clinton said. "Michiganders are proving every single day that we can still compete and win in a global economy."

Though a recent Suffolk University poll showed Clinton up by 7 points in a Michigan stop by Trump on Saturday at Great Faith

Ministries International church in Detroit as an attempt to court Black voters. This was Trump's third visit to the state since his official nomination in July. Hillary Clinton's most recent visit to Michigan was on Aug. 11, when she addressed workers at Futuramic Tool & Engineering to talk about how her economic plans are best suited for the working class.

See **CLINTON**, Page 3A

CRIME
Welcome Week data shows drop in incidents

Student hospitalizations decrease by more than 50 percent in past year

JENNIFER MEER
Daily Staff Reporter

There was over a 50 percent decrease in alcohol and drug-related hospital visits during the first five weeks of school at UM last year according to Advocate, a Domino's Life Incident database. In the first five weeks of the 2013 and 2014 fall semesters, more than 100 cases of alcohol- and drug-related hospital visits were reported to the University in Michigan through the database. In 2015, there were fifty.

There is no data available yet for 2016. Officials pointed to several reasons for the drastic change, including dry Welcome Week events, programs created by Wolverine Wellness and increased support from the Department of Public Safety and Security and other law enforcement agencies.

Beginning in the 2014 school year, the University began new initiatives to reduce student alcohol and drug use by shortening Welcome Week, the period between student move-in and the first day of class. Based on the data from Advocate, DPSS spokesperson Diane Brown said they believe the shorter Welcome Week contributed to a decline in alcohol-related emergencies.

See **HOSPITAL VISITS**, Page 3A

President Bill Clinton walks in the Labor Day parade in Detroit Monday.
AMELIA CACCHIONE/Daily

GOT A NEWS TIP?
Call 734-418-4115 or e-mail news@michigandaily.com and let us know.

For more stories and coverage, visit **michigandaily.com**

INDEX
Vol. CXXVI, No. 128
©2016 The Michigan Daily

NEWS.................2   OPINION.................4
MICHIGAN IN COLOR....5 PHOTO....................7
ARTS..................9 SPORTS TUESDAY......1B

The Michigan Daily

ONE HUNDRED AND TWENTY-FIVE YEARS OF EDITORIAL FREEDOM

Ann Arbor, Michigan | Wednesday, September 14, 2016 | michigandaily.com

The Statement
How the process of gentrification has changed Detroit's economic and social landscape
» Page 1B

The house is jumpin'
Nonprofit sets up White House bounce house on North University Ave.
» Page 3A

U.S. Sen. Tim Kaine (D-VA), Democratic vice presidential nominee, speaks to University of Michigan students and the Ann Arbor community on the Diag Tuesday.
CLAIRE ABDO/Daily

VP candidate Tim Kaine discusses student debt, gender gap at 'U' visit

Students gathered in Diag Tuesday afternoon to attend Democratic political rally

EMMA KINERY
Daily News Editor

Democratic officials encouraged Wolverines to follow their instincts and "go blue" this election Tuesday afternoon when Sen. Tim Kaine (D-VA), the Democratic vice presidential nominee, visited the University of Michigan's campus to give a speech on the Diag.

Kaine's visit marks the first time Hillary Clinton's campaign has visited campus and the vice presidential nominee's second time in the state, which went to U.S. Sen. Bernie Sanders (I-VT) in the Democratic primary, partially due to young voters. Kaine's last stop in Michigan was in early August in Grand Rapids.

Before heading to the rally on the Diag, the vice presidential nominee first went to Espresso Royale on State Street, where he met with students as well as Ann Arbor residents.

Much of Kaine's speech centered on student debt and bolstering Clinton's higher education reform plan, along with civil rights and the importance of Michigan as a swing state. Speaking before a chapter of College Democrats after Kaine's speech on the Diag Tuesday.

See **KAINE**, Page 3A

U.S. Sen. Tim Kaine (D-VA), Democratic vice presidential nominee, poses for a photo with Laura Marsh, LSA junior and vice chair of the University of Michigan's chapter of College Democrats after Kaine's speech on the Diag Tuesday.
AMANDA ALLEN/Daily

ADMINISTRATION

Study finds Mich. loan debt peaks at $29,450

University strives to balance rising tuition, financial aid

KATHERINE CURRAN
Daily Staff Reporter

Sixty-two percent of Michigan students graduate with debt of about $29,450 — making the state the ninth-highest in the nation for student debt — according to a new report from the Michigan League for Public Policy, a nonpartisan economic policy institute.

The report pointed to several possible reasons for the debt, including rising tuition and stagnant levels of federal and state aid.

Since 2003, public tuition has increased by 100 to 150 percent on average in Michigan. Meanwhile, in 2003, the Pell grant covered 40 to 66 percent of tuition. Now, the grant covers less than 40 percent at nearly all Michigan universities. At the University of Michigan specifically, in 2015, the federal Pell grant covered 26 percent of tuition.

Michigan's investment in need-based financial aid grants has also fallen since the 1990s, even amid raising tuition. The state spends less per student on

See **DEBT**, Page 3A

Author Malcolm Gladwell lectures on risks and realities of entrepreneurship

Talk hosted by Ross as part of the Joseph and Sally Handleman discussion series

EMILY PRESCOTT
Daily Staff Reporter

Author Malcolm Gladwell's lecture on the risks and realities of entrepreneurship Tuesday drew an audience large enough to fill Hill Auditorium.

The talk, which explored the careers of scientist Emil Freireich who helped invent modern chemotherapy; Steve Jobs, who founded Apple; and Ingvar Kamprad, who founded IKEA, was part of The Joseph and Sally Handleman Lecture Series hosted by the Ross School of Business.

Gladwell challenged the audience to reframe the traditional discourse surrounding entrepreneurship, encouraging them to consider the social implications as well.

"I think we spend a lot of time talking about the innovation part of entrepreneurship and not enough time talking about the social part of entrepreneurship," Gladwell said. "That's what I want to talk about this evening."

He added that entrepreneurs are defined by exigency rather than competence or resources, highlighting Jobs' attempt to produce the Macintosh computer as quickly as possible.

"That's what sets (Jobs) apart, that sense of urgency,"

Gladwell said. "That's what gives an entrepreneur their sense of direction and their sense of purpose."

He also outlined three common characteristics shared by all entrepreneurs: openness to creativity, conscientiousness and disagreeableness in terms of a disregard for the approval of others. To illustrate this notion of disagreeableness, he pointed to Freireich's struggle with the medical community's disapproval and accusations of immorality.

Despite this obstacle, Freireich continued his groundbreaking work.

"If Freireich needed approval, leukemia would still exist," he said.

Gladwell said a successful entrepreneur believes in the nature of a dynamic society, a vision which fuels the entrepreneur to implement change.

See **GLADWELL**, Page 3A

Author Malcolm Gladwell speaks as a part of the Joseph and Sally Handleman Lecture Series in Hill Auditorium Tuesday.
JEREMY MITNICK/Daily

SCIENCE

Perception of health differs for genders

Mortality risks may be connected to varying self assessments

ALEXA ST. JOHN
Daily Staff Reporter

Men and women self-rate their health differently — and this might explain in part why women live longer — according to a recent University of Michigan study.

The study found women rate themselves as less healthy more often than men, even though women tend to live longer. The study, therefore, could predict mortality better in men who viewed themselves as extremely healthy, perhaps because they were more likely not to seek medical help.

Initially designed to compare health between Black and white people, the study followed 1,500 adults ages 66 and older for three years between 2001 and 2004 and discovered that gender differences play a large role in subjectively predicting risk of mortality later in life.

"Regardless of the domain, women perceive their health being poorer — if it is mental health, if it quality of life, if it is anxiety or depression,

See **PERSONALITY**, Page 3A

GOT A NEWS TIP?
Call 734-418-4115 or e-mail news@michigandaily.com and let us know.

For more stories and coverage, visit
michigandaily.com

INDEX
Vol. CXXV, No. 134
©2016 The Michigan Daily

NEWS..............2A
OPINION..........4A
CLASSIFIEDS......6A

SUDOKU..........2A
ARTS.............5A
SPORTS...........7A

The Michigan Daily

ONE HUNDRED AND TWENTY-FIVE YEARS OF EDITORIAL FREEDOM

Ann Arbor, Michigan | Monday, September 12, 2016 | michigandaily.com

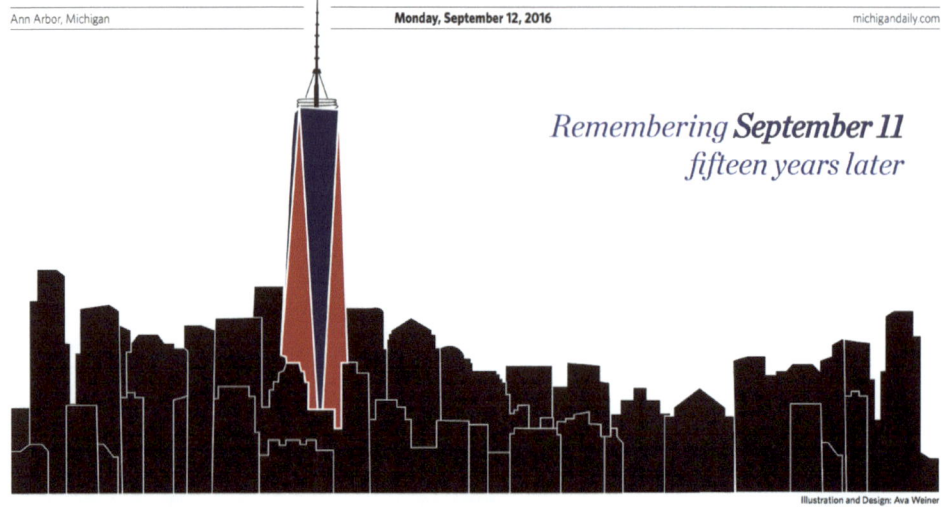

Remembering September 11
fifteen years later

Illustration and Design: Ava Weiner

Thoughts from campus: SEE PAGE 2A

AMELIA CACCHIONE/Daily
Members of the ROTC stand guard at the flagpole on the Diag on Sunday.

2,977 flags line the Diag: SEE PAGE 2A

AMELLA LALLHIUNE/Daily
American flags placed by the Young Americans for Freedom mark the 15th anniversary of 9/11 on the Diag on Sunday.

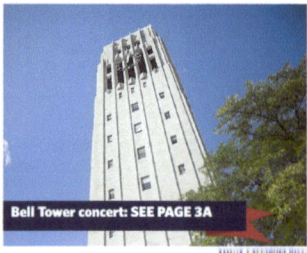

Bell Tower concert: SEE PAGE 3A

AMELIA LALLHIUNE/Daily
The School of Music, Theatre, & Dance hosted a noontime carillon recital in remembrance of 9/11 at Burton Memorial Tower on Sunday.

Terrorism abroad has not discouraged students from travel abroad programs

Summer attacks influence international experiences

JACKIE CHARNIGA
Daily Staff Editor

On August 4, Nadine Jawad, a Ford junior at the University of Michigan, received a text on the lawn of Magdalen's campus at the University of Oxford, holding her phone in one hand and playing with a piece of grass in the other. "God, my phone is blowing up because of that stabbing," she said. "It's like, I'm fine, mom."

The incident happened earlier that day in London, a city an hour and a half from Oxford by bus. The perpetrator had knifed victims indiscriminately near Russell Square. Among the five injured,
See **ABROAD**, Page 7A

one woman — an American tourist — was killed. Darlene Horton, 64, was traveling with her husband who was teaching abroad when she was killed. Other American students on the lawn, sitting next to her, started checking their phones too,

855 number of students that went abroad during 2015-16 school year

501 number of students that studied abroad in Europe

- Spain | 149
- United Kingdom | 86
- France | 76
- Denmark | 40
- Italy | 39
- Germany | 31
- Czech Republic | 27
- Netherlands | 26
- Belgium | 13
- Sweden | 8

Source: Center for Global and Intercultural Study

Fifteen years later, effects of 9/11 still apparent for University students

Lasting impacts remain in public perception

ALEXA ST. JOHN
Daily Staff Reporter

Fifteen years later, Sara Frost, School of Music, Theatre & Dance senior and New York native, remembers being picked up by her father just two hours after her first day of first grade began, on September 11, 2001.

Frost was in Manhattan on 9/11 when the al-Qaeda terrorist group coordinated a series of attacks by hijacking passenger airliners — two of which hit and later collapsed the World Trade Center North and South Towers in New York City.

Confused and unsure of what was happening, Frost and her father went to a local market on their way home.

"I have a stark memory of just rows and rows and rows of empty shelves, which was kind of crazy — it was only probably about three hours after the planes hit, they hit about 9:30 in the morning — and already the shelves were just bare," Frost said. "In terms of imagery, that's something that, just

empty shelves, has stuck with me because no one knew what was going on."

Two thousand nine hundred seventy-seven people died as a result of the attacks, including 18 alumni of the University of Michigan.

"Even though I was so young, the images that one associates, it's just really right there at the forefront of my brain, especially today."

"Even those of us who are new here, recalling our experience of the national trauma in other parts of the country, now share in the collective bereavement of the University of Michigan family," said then-University President Mary Sue Coleman at a 2002

ceremony honoring the victims. Though the attacks happened when most current University undergraduates were in elementary school, the events still have a lasting impact — for some, personally, and for others, as part of broader shifts in public perception.

"That day has always stayed really fresh and really kind of visceral in my mind," Frost said. "Even though I was so young, the images that one associates, it's just really right there at the forefront of my brain, especially today."

Beyond the personal, one of the bigger impacts of that day was on public opinion.

Following the attacks, University researchers from the Institute of Social Research found in their "How Americans Respond" survey that half of respondents were more trusting of the government in late 2001 than a year earlier, helping create attitudes reflective of increased patriotism and community among fellow citizens as well. "The HAR survey results
See **SEPTEMBER**, Page 7A

Knighted

Behind another strong offensive showing, the Michigan football team cruised to a 51-14 win over Central Florida, improving to 2-0 this season.
» Page 1B

GOT A NEWS TIP?
Call 734-418-4115 or e-mail news@michigandaily.com and let us know.

For more stories and coverage, visit **michigandaily.com**

INDEX
Vol. CXXV, No. 132
©2016 The Michigan Daily

NEWS.................2A
OPINION..............4A
ARTS.................5A

SUDOKU..............2A
CLASSIFIEDS.........5A
SPORTSMONDAY......1B

The Michigan Daily

ONE HUNDRED AND TWENTY SIX YEARS OF EDITORIAL FREEDOM

Ann Arbor, Michigan | Monday, October 10, 2016 | michigandaily.com

LOOKING BACK: THE FLINT WATER CRISIS

April 2014 — Flint begins using the Flint River as its water source instead of Detroit. Residents voice concerns about aspects of the water, including its smell, taste and color.

January 2014 — Flint leaders say the water is safe, though Detroit offers to begin providing Flint with water again.

September 24, 2014 — High levels of lead are found in children's blood and a group of doctors. State regulators say the water is safe.

September 29th, 2014 — Gov. Rick Snyder acknowledges the Flint water problem for the first time.

October 2015 — Snyder announces $1 million will be dedicated to buying water filters and to test water in Flint public schools. Soon after, he advocates for going back to Detroit's water system.

Oct. 15, 2015 — The Michigan Legislature and Snyder approve nearly $9.4 million in aid to Flint, $6 million of which will go to transitioning back to Detroit water.

Dec. 29, 2015 — Department of Environmental Quality Director Dan Wyant's resignation is accepted by Snyder, and Snyder apologizes.

Jan. 5, 2016 — Snyder declares a state of emergency in Flint. Federal officials confirm that they are investigating the crisis.

Jan. 13, 2016 — Michigan health officials report an increase in Legionnaires' disease cases over the past two years in the county that includes Flint.

March 23, 2016 — A governor-appointed panel concludes that the state of Michigan is "fundamentally accountable" for the crisis.

Aug. 14, 2016 — Flint's federal emergency declaration ends. Officials work to continue fixing the drinking water system.

Sept. 15, 2016 — $170 million water projects bill, which includes emergency funding for Flint, is approved by the U.S. Senate.

Source: Associated Press | Design: Katie Spak

One year later: Flint residents reflect on lasting impact of crisis

While high profile donations and attention have slowed, issues remain

RIYAH BASHA
Daily Staff Reporter

Flint has carried on fairly normally for MacIntyre — or as normal as it can be. Her family still drinks, bathes in and washes clothes with bottled water. Her children receive coloring pages at school reminding them to improve their nutrition and hygiene. Her home's pipes continue to disintegrate inside the walls, and daily life, she says, is rife with a lack of clarity from the government.

"We're not getting straight answers," she said in an interview. "We're scared all of the time."

A large number of Flint residents, including MacIntyre, do not believe local officials' assurances that city water is now sourced from Lake Huron through Detroit's water supply — is safe to drink, though crews of construction workers under directions from Mayor Karen Weaver are working to replace houses' piping systems. Cases of water bottles are still common sights everywhere in the city, as are citizens coping with infectious diseases; just as headlines of a deadly two-year spate of Legionnaire's disease seemed to stop, a recent outbreak of shigellosis made the news earlier this month.

Throughout the water crisis, health issues stemming from the water supply was often delayed. Government officials from Weaver to Gov. Rick Snyder (R-Mich.), all the way to President Barack Obama, who visited Flint water in bids to prove its safety.

"We have all sorts of people coming in for a hot minute," MacIntyre said in reference to the parade of activists and politicians rolling through Flint. "The story being told now, though, is that we're fine."

For residents, what's most toxic in the city runs deeper than any network of pipes, and can't be fixed by chemical treatments — many say over the last two years, they've lost what little trust remained in city and state government.

Local activist Nayyirah Shariff cited demographics in explaining the bleak conclusion she and her neighbors have reached about Flint, where 67 percent of residents are Black and 40 percent live under the poverty line.

"It's a dangerous public policy model," she said. "If you're poor, you lose access to democracy."

What went wrong
The timeline of the water crisis,

See FLINT, Page 3A

Professors and students work to find houses with lead pipes

Google and University of Michigan partner to find vulnerable locations

BRIAN KUANG
Daily Staff Reporter

When approached by Google and the University of Michigan-Flint to collaborate on a mobile app advising Flint residents on lead risk levels in their homes, assistant prof. of Engineering Jacob Abernethy and Business prof. Eric Schwartz saw both a critical gap between available data and the city's recovery efforts — and a way to fix it.

Of the approximately 35,000 occupied structures in Flint, only about 7 to 10 percent are estimated to be affected by lead contamination, largely due to the usage of private water service lines with lead in the pipes which connect individual homes to city-wide water mains.

However, Schwartz said records on service line composition were incomplete, tests were unreliable and no specific pattern of lead contamination could be discerned from maps.

See DATA, Page 2A

STATE
$4.1 million grant for Detroit raises questions

University students and professor express concerns over local impact

MATT HARMON
Daily Staff Reporter

The U.S. Department of Commerce announced last Monday that the city of Detroit and the Detroit Economic Growth Corporation, a nonprofit organization consisting of public authorities that manage economic development efforts in the city, will receive a $4.1 million grant to improve the I-94 Industrial Park on the city's east side.

City officials, including Detroit Mayor Mike Duggan and Detroit City Councilmember Scott Benson, have stated these efforts are meant to attract manufacturers to the industrial park and create more jobs for Detroiters. However, research conducted by Margaret Dewar, professor of Urban Planning at the Taubman College of Architecture and Urban planning, has cited that the jobs are not guaranteed to eligible local workers — a concern echoed by University of Michigan students from Detroit.

The grant allocates $910,000 for the hiring of an Economic Recovery Coordination Team to oversee industrial site renovations and support manufacturing branches making the move to Detroit. Additionally, almost $3.2 million is slated for renovations to redevelop and expand Georgia Street, a key access point in the area that could be utilized by large trucks to ship goods.

Dewar said the money does come with notable positives, noting that the city would benefit from having the federal government front the amount for the infrastructure, and that the grant is capable of creating positive effects for Detroit's immediate economy.

"I think it's terrific that the city got that grant because what has to happen is that industrial park is that the infrastructure needs to be updated," Dewar

See DETROIT, Page 3A

More than 2,000 participate in eighth MHacks competition

Student-run event features wide range of tech. projects

KEVIN LINDER
Daily Staff Reporter

Hackers from all over the country gathered in downtown Detroit on Saturday to code, design, collaborate and invent for MHacks 8, a 36-hour event run by University of Michigan students. Part of Major League Hacking, a national collegiate hackathon league, the event provides a platform for individuals to come together to build or code projects within the 36-hour period.

According to event organizers, about 2,000 people attended —

See MHACKS, Page 3A

MHacks participants begin creating their projects, which will be completed in 36 hours, at midnight Friday at the Masonic Temple in Detroit. GRANT HARDY/Daily

---

FOOTBALL
Wolverines lay historic beatdown on Rutgers

No. 4 Michigan scores 11 touchdowns, goes for two on one in 78-0 win

MAX BULTMAN
Managing Sports Editor

PISCATAWAY — There was a turning point, Jim Harbaugh said. That's not something you often hear in a game like Saturday's. In fact, it's not often you see a game like Saturday's.

The Michigan football team scored 78 points, twice the number of total yards it allowed to Rutgers. In case it doesn't go without saying, the Wolverines shut out the Scarlet Knights (0-3 Big Ten, 2-4 overall) on their own field Saturday, winning 78-0 and driving out a heavy majority of the fans well before the final whistle.

But about that turning point. Harbaugh said it came when Jabrill Peppers — his redshirt sophomore

See FOOTBALL, Page 3A

Jersey Score
Jabrill Peppers found the end zone twice in his homecoming game, and Michigan rolled to a 78-0 rout in Piscataway.
» Page 1B

GOT A NEWS TIP?
Call 734-418-4115 or e-mail news@michigandaily.com and let us know.

For more stories and coverage, visit **michigandaily.com**

INDEX | Vol. CXXVI, No. 8 | ©2016 The Michigan Daily
NEWS.........2A SUDOKU........2A
OPINION......4A ARTS..........5A
CLASSIFIEDS..5A SPORTSMONDAY..1B

The Michigan Daily

ONE HUNDRED AND TWENTY-SIX YEARS OF EDITORIAL FREEDOM

Ann Arbor, Michigan — Tuesday, April 18, 2017 — michigandaily.com

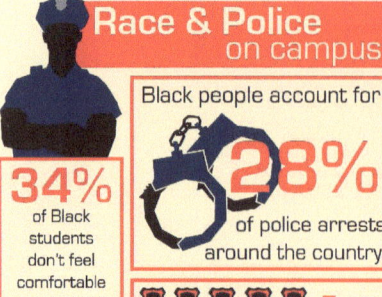

DESIGN BY NOAH SHERRIN

Black students outline concerns with issues of overpolicing in A²

Members of the Black community highlight negative encounters with law enforcement

RIYAH BASHA & ALLANA AKHTAR
Daily News Editor & Daily Staff Reporter

University of Michigan student Dyshon Toxey doesn't smile much anymore.

An LSA senior, Toxey is finishing his degree in cognitive science and mathematics, is involved in a number of development programs for fellow first-generation students. Toxey is Black, and said he often took pride in his perfectly straight, groomed set of teeth to build connections in Black circles and beyond — he's known as a community mentor with an easygoing demeanor and an even easier smile.

That is, he was until last April, when Toxey was detained, body slammed and handcuffed outside Hill Auditorium for alleged disorderly conduct at the SpringFest concert headlined by Migos.

Toxey recounted event staff asking him and his friends — all Black students — to fill in the front rows of the concert, then being asked by security guards to leave shortly thereafter. When a white Ann Arbor police officer attempted to grab ahold of him, Toxey, who admits he was intoxicated, said he had no one to protect me, no one was videotaping. I really was not trying to get into an altercation."

When Toxey came to a stop near the Panera on North University Avenue, he said the officer threw him to the ground and kneed him in the back, knocking a tooth out and spraining Toxey's wrist in the process. Toxey said he was later transported to the University Hospital and released hours later, with stitches, crutches and a bill totaling nearly $7,000 in medical fees. The University's Division of Public Safety and Safety notes the case as closed in its crime log. Toxey, the report details, was taken to the emergency room for "treatment of injuries sustained during a fall when he was fleeing."

Despite protests from his parents, Toxey didn't inquire into his record; he wanted to brush the incident aside, take his final exams and return to his family and home in Harlem, New York. He said he was never notified about his charges again.

"(The cop) kept saying, 'I told you not to run,'" Toxey said. "'I told you not to run.' And then I never heard anything from them again."

A few other Black students who were present at the concert corroborate Toxey's account, but they agree on more than just his take on the night's events. Toxey's fate was not surprising to them. The Black community on campus and in Ann Arbor, many students claim, is more frequently and aggressively policed in student life than other demographics at the University. More stringent law enforcement, then, does little to close the gap between Black students' lived outside of the classroom and mainstream perceptions of the glorified Michigan experience.

Many lament that few qualifiers can spare Black students, especially Black men. For all of LSA freshman Rashan Gary's acclaim as a highly recruited defensive tackle on the football team, he said he witnessed similar stereotyping while interviewing an Ann Arbor Police Department officer for a class project on community relations. The cop said, if he had seen Gary, 6'5" feet tall and 287 pounds, on the street late at night without context, he'd have reason to be scared.

"He was straight up about it, that I could be dangerous or something," Gary said.

The suspicion is often institutionalized. As recently as two weeks ago, in a carjacking case in downtown Ann Arbor, AAPD Detective Lt. Matt Lige told MLive the suspect was described as "a light-skinned black male." The department arrested a white 17 year old for the crime three days later. Elizabeth James, program associate director of the Department of Afroamerican and African Studies, pointed to the mistaken identity case as a microcosm of larger systemic issues in local forces. The discrepancy in policing, she said, is something she's been aware of since she began working in Ann Arbor in the early '90s.

"What do we do with our tall men ... or our darker men?" she asked.

"There's a double consciousness for Black students that's always resting on your shoulder. Your party's going to be shut down ... even when it's in the (Michigan) Union. You've got to walk more delicately, and you have to be twice as good."

I. The Danger in Numbers

In the years since Michael Brown's death at the hands of a police officer in Ferguson, Mo., Black departments across the country have come under fire for both aggressive tactics and racial disparity. A New York Times study in 2015 found white representation in hundreds of police forces across the country is up to more than 30 percentage points higher than their community's proportion of white residents.

Ann Arbor wasn't spared from the slew of fatal police shootings. In 2014, a Black woman named Aura Rosser, who suffered from mental health issues, was killed by white AAPD officer David Ried — county prosecutors later refused to indict Ried for what officials deemed lawful self-defense. Rosser's death sparked protests and prompted AAPD to mandate body cameras and diversity training, but the force hasn't yet collected data on whether its demographics have shifted. As of the last Bureau of Justice Statistics survey in 2013, 82.8 percent of sworn AAPD officers were white, more than 10 percent higher than the percentage of Ann Arbor residents who were white.

At the University, police demographics bear striking resemblance to national forces. White officers and staff members represent 78.1 percent of DPSS, which includes University Police, Housing Security, Michigan Medicine Security and general Security Services. Only 10.7 percent of DPSS is Black, while 4.6 percent is Latino. Furthermore, the division is overwhelmingly male, with women making up just 32.8 percent of DPSS.

II. Hands in the Air

Most students' interactions with police at the University take place against the backdrop of parties, with the ubiquity of underage drinking

See POLICE, Page 3

ANN ARBOR

High rise to be built at Ann Arbor Library Lot

City Council passes the resolution to sell lot despite community division on sale

ISHI MORI
Daily Staff Reporter

Concerned citizens filled Larcom City Hall Monday night as the Ann Arbor City Council voted to authorize the sale of the Library Lot, a piece of real estate across from the downtown Ann Arbor District Library on Fifth Avenue, to Chicago developer Core Spaces. Core Spaces, a firm centered around real estate management, is set to build a high-rise at the location.

The council's decision concluded a decade-long struggle for the future of the Library Lot, which is currently a city-owned surface parking space. Public opinion has been divided between constructing a $10 million, 17-story, multipurpose high-rise — which is the current plan — and setting aside the land as a public common area with a few small-scale residential projects.

Councilmember Chuck Warpehoski (D-Ward 5) said a new building would provide several benefits in the long run by contributing $5 million in revenue from the high-rise to the Affordable Housing Fund, aiding the local.

See LIBRARY LOT, Page 3

Hidden Gems: A look at three libraries on the University of Michigan's campus

Preservation and digitization efforts are priorities at the Bentley, Clements and Ford

ALEXA ST. JOHN
Managing News Editor

It was a dismal, Michigan morning — cloudy, with raindrops that didn't warrant the use of an umbrella but were heavy enough for me to put up my sweatshirt hood — and it was my first semester. I went to the Bentley Historical Library on North Campus for the first time. I had been forced into familiarity with the buses going to the University's separate campus — I had an 8:30 a.m. class on North four days a week and knew how to navigate the often daunting system. I arrived at the library after a quick trip on one such bus.

The Bentley Library — established in 1935 by the University Board of Regents — had archives I needed to see for one of my earliest stories at the Daily. I was working on a piece about the newly archived collection of University alum Jack Kevorkian, a famed advocate for assisted suicide. What I found in the archives, procured by library assistants, were files of what are referred to as "medicide" — or medically assisted suicide — letters Kevorkian received from clients whom were suffering from illnesses they believed made their lives unbearable. There were also records from Kevorkian's court trials; following years of advocacy, he was convicted and sent to prison for murder.

At the time these papers and files were made available to the public in December 2015, Lara Zielin, the editorial director at the Bentley Historical Library, said an increase in interest in the archives was noticeable.

"It's a sensitive subject, and we're aware it evokes lots of strong feelings," Zielin said at the time. "We're trying to be respectful and cautious about the material while, at the same time, not withholding the things that his estate wanted public."

These archives are just a fraction of 11,000 other research collections at the library — from those of University administrators to University athletics to documentation of Detroit's history and state legislature phones — with more than 25,000 digital images scanned in its image bank, all geared toward serving as official preservation at the Bentley, the William L. Clements and the Gerald R. Ford Presidential libraries at the University —

See ARCHIVES, Page 3

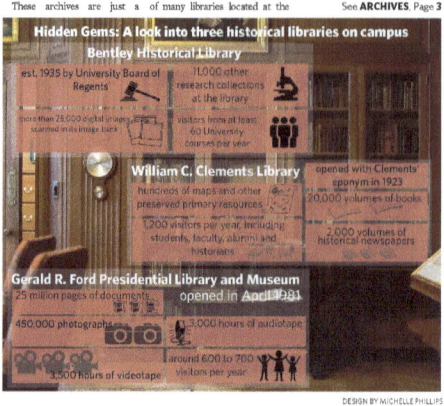

GOVERNMENT

Website for contacting politicians developed

LSA student initiates "Going Postal Politics" to send postcards to reps

CARLY RYAN
Daily Staff Reporter

Inspired by political involvement on campus, LSA junior Alexander Forsyth has developed a website to help expedite the process of sending mail to politicians.

The website, called Going Postal Politics, aims to reduce the tedious process of sending mail in three steps: pick from pre-made postcards, choose which politician to send the postcard to and send it for 99 cents. Users also have the opportunity to upload their own photos for postcards.

The site asserts that postcards are the most effective way to deliver a message to politicians because of their simplicity and visual effect. The postcards feature many of the issues students on campus have been fighting for, such as the Black Lives Matter Movement, #NoDAPL and the immigration ban.

"Most of the inspiration comes from students or activist Twitter," Forsyth said. "I've been paying attention."

See WEBSITE, Page 3

The Michigan Daily

ONE HUNDRED AND TWENTY-SIX YEARS OF EDITORIAL FREEDOM

Ann Arbor, Michigan — Wednesday, March 8, 2017 — michigandaily.com

BLACK STUDENT ENROLLMENT — BY THE NUMBERS

- Of **19,338** LSA students
- there are **11,694** white students
- and **961** black students
- LESS THAN **1** black student to every **1,000** white
- **607** black female students to **10,529** white in LSA
- for men, **354** black students / **5,294** white males in LSA
- black enrollment dropped from **5.1%** in 2015 to **4.6%** in 2016

DESIGN BY: MICHELLE PHILLIPS

ACADEMICS

Civil rights attorney given medal for activism

Acclaimed criminal justice lawyer Bryan Stevenson received the Wallenberg Medal

RIYAH BASHA & TIM COHN
Daily News Editors

Acclaimed criminal justice attorney Bryan Stevenson received the University of Michigan Wallenberg Medal Tuesday evening at a packed Rackham Auditorium filled with more than 1,000 attendees. Stevenson, the head of the Equal Justice Initiative and author of best-selling memoir "Just Mercy," delivered a keynote address narrating his experiences in criminal justice reform and urging attendees to craft hopeful narratives.

According to John Godfrey, assistant dean for international education at the Rackham

Graduate School and member of the medal selection committee, the Wallenberg Medal is an annual award given to a person who demonstrates a commitment to human rights.

"We look for someone who has upheld the values of Raoul Wallenberg," Godfrey said. "Someone who is outspoken in the defense of human rights, who has put himself or herself in the front lines for justice protecting those who are oppressed and who have really sought to make a difference in the world."

Previous winners of the Wallenberg Medal include Russian journalist Masha Gessen, an outspoken Putin critic; U.S. Rep. John Lewis (D-Ga), a civil

See MEDAL, Page 3A

Black community responds to DPS applicants' fear of discrimination

Renaissance High School student published an OpEd on racism before experiencing the 'U'

JACKIE CHARNIGA
Daily Staff Reporter

Cydney Gardner-Brown, a recently accepted applicant to the University of Michigan, is having difficulty deciding whether she wants to be a Wolverine. The debate does not center around the price of admission or housing, nor is she concerned about leaving home for the first time. Gardner-Brown is more concerned about her safety as a Black student.

In an op-ed published in the RHS Stentor – Renaissance High School's student news publication – titled "Should I fear attending the University of Michigan?"

Gardner-Brown investigates the emotional cost in adjusting from a predominantly Black high school to a predominantly white campus – a transition she describes as "going off to spaces without guarantee of our safety."

The Stentor is part of Dialogue, a quarterly publication that incorporates student contributions from several Detroit high schools. It is jointly supported by Crain Communications, a Detroit-based publishing conglomerate, and the Michigan State University School of Journalism.

In the article, Gardner-Brown cites recent events including the hacking of Computer Science Prof.

See APPLICANT, Page 3A

CAMPUS LIFE

Panel talks reactions of Latino community

The speakers discussed policy, uncertainties under Trump administration

JORDYN BAKER
Daily Staff Reporter

"Pa'Delante" is a saying often used in Latino communities. In English translation it's commonly translated to mean "pick yourself up, dust yourself off, and keep moving forward." This type of resilience was a prevailing theme among speakers at a panel hosted Tuesday evening discussing immigration, specifically for the Latino community and in relation to recent immigration policies set by President Donald Trump.

Nearly 50 students, faculty and community members gathered to hear from five panelists with experiences including working with and assisting immigrants, providing employment with seasonal and migrant workers and studying healthy equity within immigrant communities.

Panelist Rudy Flores, co-chair of the Migrant Resource Council of Southeast Michigan, explained that in the past 48 hours in his town of Adrian, there have been three different ICE raids. In which raids, three people were detained.

"These are situations that we anticipated but didn't expect,"

See PANEL, Page 3A

Hundreds attend Lambda Chi Alpha fraternity's vigil in memory of brother

The community gathered to celebrate life and accomplishments of Peter Hart

COLIN BERESFORD
Daily Staff Reporter

Lambda Chi Alpha fraternity held a candlelight vigil Tuesday night in honor of their brother, Peter Hart, who took his own life in February before Spring Break. Hundreds gathered on the front lawn of the fraternity to share stories and remember Hart.

LSA sophomore Daniel Greene, president of Lambda Chi Alpha and Hart's social big, spoke to the group gathered on the front lawn in memory of Hart.

"Peter Hart will always be loved, will always be missed," Greene said. "But as his big, as his president, as his friend, most importantly as his brother, I ask that you continue his legacy in challenging yourself to be slightly more honest with the world; to be slightly more open-minded."

LSA sophomore Michael Wysong, a member of the Sigma Kappa fraternity, attended the vigil to show support for other members of Greek life and his friends who knew Hart personally.

"I think it's affecting us really hard since a lot of ... guys deal with depression, so we all just want to let everyone know that you can always talk to someone," Wysong said. "It's basically

a way just for everyone to realize that there's always someone next to you."

LSA freshman Anna Fedder said she has been in shock since hearing of Hart's passing.

"I saw him ... two weeks ago, or something like that, just walking around, on my way back from class," Fedder said.

"It's tough. I wish I had known more, I guess ... but obviously you can't go back and fix that."

LSA junior Andrew Sharon, a brother at the fraternity, said since Hart's passing, members of the Lambda Chi Alpha fraternity have been trying to process the tragedy, celebrating Hart's membership in the fraternity and knowing him.

"Obviously everyone is really upset," Sharon said. "But more importantly, we're happy we had Peter around. He was always the most committed. I live at the house now and he was always at the house more than I was. He literally just wanted to be in everything – he ran for positions, he was always at every party, every event, every brotherhood event."

Brothers of the Lambda Chi Alpha fraternity gather for a candlelight vigil in honor of Peter Hart at the Lambda Chi Alpha chapter house on Tuesday.

HALEY MCLAUGHLIN/Daily

STUDENT GOVERNMENT

CSG body supports Elections as holiday

The resolution hopes to increase student voter outcome in future years

RHEA CHEETI
Daily Staff Reporter

A resolution to support an academic holiday on Election Day for 2020 and all even-numbered years after that passed during Tuesday night's Central Student Government meeting with 30 in favor, five opposed and none abstaining. The resolution faced pushback from some representatives, who said the resolution only featured the views of students in CSG and wasn't reflective of the student body in general.

While introducing the resolution, Engineering freshman Mario Galindez, a member of the Engineering Student Government, talked about how voter turnout has historically been much lower in student-populated areas as compared to more residential, non-student populations.

He also mentioned how long lines, especially in areas like the Michigan Union, were caused by the lack of student and faculty volunteers who could have aided the process. These individuals could have helped, however, if they had the day off.

See CSG, Page 3A

GOT A NEWS TIP?
Call 734-418-4115 or e-mail

For more stories and coverage, visit

INDEX
Vol. CXXVII, No. 40

NEWS 2
OPINION ......

SUDOKU 2
CLASSIFIEDS ...

ABOUT

Francesca Kielb was the 2016 Managing Design Editor for *The Michigan Daily*. As both a designer and a writer, her interest in publication design stemmed from her desire to communicate compelling ideas, be they written or visual. She is now living in Chicago and continuing to find ways to merge these modes of expression.